CHECK YOUR ENGLISH VOCABULARY FOR

TOEFL®

Editor and Contributor

Rawdon Wyatt

(For first edition)

Editor

Liz Greasby

Contributors

Mark Aston

THE FRIARY
LEARNING CENTRE

www.bloomsbury.com

First published in Great Britain 2002

This second edition published in 2004
Reprinted 2005
Bloomsbury Publishing Plc
38 Soho Square, London, W1D 3HB

British Library Cataloguing in Publication Data
A catalogue entry for this book is available from the British Library
ISBN: 0 7475 6984 3

Text computer typeset by Bloomsbury Publishing
Printed in Italy by Legoprint

All papers used by Bloomsbury Publishing are natural, recyclable products made from wood

grown in well-managed forests. The manufacturing processes conform to the environmental

regulations of the country of origin.

TOEFL® Test is a registered trademark of Educational Testing Service (ETS).
This publication is not endorsed or approved by ETS

Introduction

If you are going to take the TOEFL® test, you will find the vocabulary exercises in this workbook very helpful. They will help you to review, practice and acquire a lot of the words and expressions that you might need to use in the Writing section (and, from 2005, the Speaking section), or that you might come across or be tested on in the Listening, Reading and Structure sections. A greater command of vocabulary is one of the key factors that will help you raise your TOEFL® Test score.

Structure of the workbook

The workbook is divided into 2 sections. The first section deals with general vocabulary, including synonyms, idioms and phrasal verbs. The second section is topic-specific, and focuses on some of the topics that regularly appear in the TOEFL® test. Each topic is accompanied by a typical TOEFL® Writing question, which will give you the chance to use the key vocabulary in an essay.

There is an answer key at the back of the book.

How to use the book

You should not go through the exercises mechanically. It is better to choose areas that you are unfamiliar with, or areas that you feel are of specific interest or importance to yourself.

Remember that you should keep a record of new words and expressions that you learn, and review these from time to time so that they become an active part of your vocabulary. There is a vocabulary record sheet at the back of the book which you can photocopy as many times as you like. Use this to build up your own personal vocabulary bank.

It is essential to have a good dictionary with you when you are doing the exercises. For basic vocabulary, we recommend the *American English Study Dictionary* published by Bloomsbury Plc (ISBN 1-901659-69-0).

Extending your vocabulary

Also remember that there are other methods of acquiring new vocabulary. For example, you should read as much as possible from a different variety of authentic reading materials (books, newspapers, magazines, etc).

Information about the TOEFL® Test.

The purpose of the TOEFL® Test is to evaluate a non-native English speaker's proficiency in the English language. Almost one million students every year from 180 countries register to take the TOEFL® Test: the majority of universities and colleges in North America as well as in other English-speaking countries require official TOEFL® Test score reports for admission. The test is also used by institutions in other countries where English is the language of instruction. In addition, government agencies, scholarship programs and licensing / certification agencies use TOEFL® Test scores to evaluate English proficiency. An acceptable score depends on the particular institution or agency involved.

Introduction

TOEFL® Test programs

There are three TOEFL® testing programs: the **Supplemental Paper-Based TOEFL® Test**, the **Computer-Based TOEFL® Test** and the **Institutional TOEFL® Test**.

The *Supplemental Paper-Based TOEFL® Test* and the *Computer-Based TOEFL® Test* are both official administrations. The *Institutional TOEFL® Test* is not an official administration and is used for admission, placement or employment only at the school or agency offering the test.

The *Computer-Based TOEFL®* (CBT), which was introduced in July 1998 in many parts of the world, combines many of the question types used in the traditional paper-based test with new question types that can be offered only on the computer. The *Supplemental Paper-Based TOEFL® Test* program is a paper and pencil version of the TOEFL® Test, which was reintroduced temporarily to replace mobile computer testing in a few remote places. When the *Computer-Based TOEFL® Test* is phased in for your area you must take the *Computer-Based TOEFL® Test*, as all paper-based TOEFL® tests will be gradually replaced.

You can find further information and order a TOEFL® Test Information Bulletin if you visit the official website at www.toefl.org.

All TOEFL® Test programs test the same four language skills – listening, structure, writing and reading – in three separate sections:

Section 1: **Listening**
Section 2: **Structure/Writing**
Section 3: **Reading**

The *Computer-Based TOEFL® Test* has a **Writing** section in which you have to write a short essay on a topic assigned by the computer from a pool of topics. The **Listening** and **Structure** sections are **'computer-adaptive'** in the *Computer-Based TOEFL® Test*, i.e. only one question appears on the screen, and everyone does not receive the same questions. Questions are chosen from a very large pool of questions, categorized by difficulty and content and based on how you answer the previous questions. For instance, the first question you receive in a computer-adaptive section will be of average difficulty. If you answer it correctly you are given a more difficult question; if you answer it incorrectly you are given an easier one. You receive more points for answering difficult questions correctly than you do for answering average or easy questions correctly.

The **Reading** section of the test is **not adaptive**. This section is similar to that of the paper-based test in that you will receive passages and accompanying sets of questions. Because the selection of these passages and questions will not be based on your performance, you will be allowed to omit items or go back to previous questions.

If you have little experience with computers, there is a **Tutorial** at the beginning of the *Computer-Based TOEFL® Test* to help you become familiar with using a mouse, scrolling and answering all the question types on the test.

The *Supplemental Paper-Based TOEFL® Test* and the *Institutional TOEFL® Test* are different from the *Computer-Based TOEFL® Test* because the test designs are different. The paper-based TOEFL tests are **linear** tests, i.e. all the questions appear in a row and everyone receives the same questions. The *Supplemental Paper-Based TOEFL® Test* does not have a composition section if you take the TOEFL® Test in August, October, December, February or May. You will also have to take the **TWE (Test of Written English)** and you may have to take the **TSE (Test of Spoken English)** if you apply for positions as teaching assistants or certification in the health professions.

The **test design** for both the paper- and the computer-based tests assures that all test takers will be tested on similar skills (e.g. comprehension of main idea, understanding of inferences) and subject matter (a variety of topics for lectures and passages).

v

Introduction

The Sections of the TOEFL® Test

The three sections of TOEFL® Test four language skills.

Listening measures the ability to understand short conversations and longer talks in English as it is spoken in North America. This section tests comprehension of main ideas, supporting ideas, important details, and inferences. You will both see and hear the questions before the answer choices appear.

Structure measures the ability to recognize language that is appropriate for standard written English. The language tested is formal, rather than conversational. When topics have a national context, they refer to US or Canadian history, culture, art, or literature. However, knowledge of these contexts is not needed to answer the questions.

Reading measures the ability to understand short passages similar in topic and style to academic texts used in North American colleges and universities. You will read a variety of short passages on academic subjects and answer several questions about each passage.

Writing measures the ability to write in English on an assigned topic. This includes the ability to generate and organize ideas, to support these ideas with examples or evidence, and to compose in standard written English a response to the assigned topic. You will not have a choice of topics and you **must write on the topic you are assigned.** You must choose whether to type your essay on the computer or to handwrite on the answer sheet provided.

Timetable for the Computer-Based TOEFL® Test

Tutorial		
(Untimed)	Computer Skills	7 tutorials
Section 1		
(40–60 minutes)	Listening	30–50 questions
Section 2: Part One		
(15–20 minutes)	Structure	20–25 questions
Break (5 minutes)		
Section 3		
(70–90 minutes)	Reading	44–55 questions
Section 2: Part Two		
(30 minutes)	Essay	1 question

Total time: 4.5 hours

Timetable for the Supplemental Paper-Based TOEFL® Test

Section 1		
(40 minutes)	Listening Comprehension	50 questions
Section 2		
(25 minutes)	Structure & Written Expression	40 questions
Section 3		
(55 minutes)	Reading Comprehension	50 questions
TWE		
(30 minutes)	Essay	1 question

Total time: 3 hours

Contents

General Vocabulary

This section deals with general vocabulary, including synonyms, idioms and phrasal verbs

Word formation: nouns

Many verbs can be changed to nouns by adding extra letters to the end of the word (e.g. *-ation, -ion, -ment*) or by changing other features of the word. Making sure that you know the different forms of the words you learn is a fast way to expand your English vocabulary.

Exercise 1. The words in this list are all verbs. What are the noun forms? Write them in the second column. The first one has been done for you as an example.

1. abolish   *abolition*

2. achieve   _____

3. commit   _____

4. disagree   _____

5. emphasize   _____

6. fail   _____

7. gain   _____

8. illustrate   _____

9. justify   _____

10. modernize   _____

11. object   _____

12. postpone   _____

13. refuse   _____

14. speculate   _____

Exercise 2. First, check your answers to Exercise 1 in the key. Then rewrite the sentences below using nouns instead of verbs. Do not change the meanings of the sentences. The first one has been done for you as an example.

1. The vice principal was modest about what he had achieved at the college.

    The vice principal was modest about _____ *his achievements at the college* _____

2. We requested that the meeting be postponed until next week.

    We requested the _____

3. The book is illustrated with color pictures of the birds.

    The book has color _____

4. The interviewee didn't get the job because he refused to wear a suit.

    The interviewee didn't get the job due to his _____

Word formation: nouns

5. The two examiners disagreed over who should get the best grade.

   The two examiners had a _____

6. The tutor emphasized the importance of completing the assignment.

   The tutor placed great _____

7. Dennis failed in his first attempt.

   Dennis's first attempt was _____

8. The dollar gained five cents on the foreign exchange markets.

   The dollar made a _____

9. The presidential candidate committed himself to lowering taxes.

   The presidential candidate made _____

10. Would you object to my smoking?

    Do you have any _____

11. The spokesperson justified the tax rise as an effort to increase welfare funds.

    Increasing welfare funds was the spokesperson's _____

12. The press are speculating that the governor will resign.

    There is _____

13. When the party was modernized, it attracted more voters.

    More voters were attracted to the party when it underwent _____

14. When was the slave trade abolished?

    When did the _____

Don't forget to keep a record of the words and expressions that you have learned, review your notes from time to time and try to use new vocabulary items whenever possible.

© Bloomsbury Publishing. For reference see *American English Study Dictionary* (1-901659-69-0)

Word formation: adjectives

Studying the different forms of each word you learn is a good way of building your vocabulary. In this exercise you will be using the adjective forms of selected nouns. The *italicized* words in the sentences in *Column A* are all nouns. What are the adjective forms? Complete the sentences in *Column B* using the correct adjective forms. Remember that common adjective endings include: -*ful*, -*ry*, and –*ous*. The first question has been done for you as an example.

Column A

1. Henry had a lot of **experience** in business matters.

2. **Helpfulness** is very much a part of Barbara's character.

3. The student's second comment was a direct **contradiction** of his first statement.

4. The Professor's report was the source of much **controversy.**

5. The government had the **determination** to carry through the legislation.

6. The firefighter couldn't enter the room because of the **intensity** of the flames.

7. There is plenty of **space** in the garage.

8. The expansion of the Internet has brought great **prosperity** to the US economy.

9. Greg didn't have much **enthusiasm** for his schoolwork.

10. The President enjoyed huge **popularity** until the welfare system collapsed.

Column B

1. Henry was very *experienced in business matters* .

2. Barbara is very _____ _____.

3. The student's two statements were _____ _____.

4. The Professor's report was very _____ _____.

5. The government was _____ _____.

6. The firefighter couldn't enter the room because the flames were too _____ _____.

7. The garage is really _____ _____.

8. The expansion of the Internet has made the US economy _____ _____ .

9. Greg wasn't very _____ _____.

10. The President was extremely _____ _____.

Opposites of adjectives

You will probably find it easier to assimilate new vocabulary for the TOEFL® Test if you learn words in related groups, rather than in isolation. It makes sense, therefore, to learn pairs of opposites together.

Many adjectives can be made into their opposite form by adding prefixes (e.g. dis-, il-, im-, in-, ir-, un-). Unfortunately, there are very few rules to tell you which adjectives take which prefixes; you have to learn each one individually. It is worth remembering, however, that the most common prefix is un-.

Exercise 1. Make the opposites of these adjectives by adding prefixes. The first one has been done for you as an example.

1. _____ un _____ likely

2. _____ logical

3. _____ appropriate

4. _____ responsible

5. _____ patient

6. _____ possible

7. _____ honest

8. _____ expected

9. _____ regular

10. _____ convincing

11. _____ proper

12. _____ certain

13. _____ active

14. _____ literate

15. _____ relevant

16. _____ satisfied

17. _____ fortunate

18. _____ obedient

19. _____ accessible

20. _____ legal

Don't forget to keep a record of the words and expressions that you have learned, review your notes from time to time and try to use new vocabulary items whenever possible.

5

Opposites of adjectives

Exercise 2. Complete these sentences using the opposites from Exercise 1. The first one has been done for you as an example.

1. The resignation of the vice president was most _____*unexpected*_____ – she seemed to be enjoying the job so much.

2. Cindy was _____ with her job and decided to start looking for a new one.

3. The volcano has been _____ for many centuries. Whether it will remain so for much longer is a source of great debate amongst vulcanologists.

4. It is _____ to sell liquor without a license.

5. The student was _____ to leave the lecture. He needed to meet a friend at the other end of the campus.

6. Many employers in the media regard Media Studies as _____ to the day-to-day workings of the industry.

7. It's _____ to greet a Japanese businessman with a kiss.

8. The only way to enter the lecture theatre was via the staircase, making it _____ for students with disabilities.

9. Most self-respecting scientists would consider it _____ to turn base metal into gold.

10. With so few schools or teachers, it is hardly surprising that so many children are _____.

11. Richie had only one more question to answer in the exam. It was therefore _____ that his pen ran out of ink.

12. The doctor was _____ as to whether the operation would benefit the patient.

Extension. Work with a partner and test each other. One partner closes the book, while the other asks questions such as 'What's the opposite of likely?'

Word formation: verbs

Learning words that are related in structure is an effective way of building your vocabulary. Exercise 1 will familiarize you with nouns and verbs that have the same stem, and Exercise 2 will give you practice in using some of these verbs.

Exercise 1. The words listed in the table below are nouns. What are the verb forms of these nouns? The first question has been done for you as an example.

1. allowance _____ *allow* _____
2. experiment _____
3. arrangement _____
4. illustration _____
5. calculation _____
6. collison _____
7. celebration _____
8. involvement _____
9. development _____
10. limitation _____

11. diagnosis _____
12. maintenance _____
13. disapproval _____
14. omission _____
15. endorsement _____
16. prediction _____
17. examination _____
18. recovery _____
19. exclusion _____
20. submission _____

Exercise 2. Choose ten verbs from Exercise 1 and write a sentence below for each one. Write the correct form of each verb in the column on the right and leave gaps for the verbs in the sentences. Cover up the right-hand column and give the sentences to another student as a test. For example:

He _____ his fiftieth birthday with an expensive party_____ celebrated

1. _____ _____
2. _____ _____
3. _____ _____
4. _____ _____
5. _____ _____
6. _____ _____
7. _____ _____
8. _____ _____
9. _____ _____
10. _____ _____

7

Prefixes

Many English words consist of more than one part. Identifying different word parts can help you to determine the meaning of words that you do not understand in the TOEFL® Test. The exercises on pages 7–8 look at how you can make opposites of some adjectives by adding on other letters. It is also possible to identify other prefixes that add meaning to the base word or word root. Some common prefixes are shown in the table below:

Prefix	Meaning	Examples
auto-	self	autobiography, autonomy
circum-	around	circumference, circumvent
co-	with, together	cohabit, cohesion
inter-	between, among	interstate, intermission
micro-	small	microorganism, microscope
mono-	one, single	monopoly, monosyllable
post-	later than, after	posthumous, postpone
pre-	before	precondition, predetermine
sub-	under	submarine, subordinate
trans-	across	transatlantic, transmit
uni-	one	unify, unique

Define each of the examples in the table. The first one has been done for you as an example:

autobiography	=	*story of the life of a person written by himself or herself*
autonomy	=	
circumference	=	
circumvent	=	
cohabit	=	
cohesion	=	
interstate	=	
intermission	=	
microorganism	=	
microscope	=	
monopoly	=	
monosyllable	=	
posthumous	=	
postpone	=	
precondition	=	
predetermine	=	
submarine	=	
subordinate	=	
transatlantic	=	
transmit	=	
unify	=	
unique	=	

© Bloomsbury Publishing. For reference see *American English Study Dictionary* (1-901659-69-0)

There are 15 nouns in the box below. Use them to complete the sentences. The first one has been done for you as an example.

addiction •	bulletin •	charisma •	constitution •	dignitary
facet •	fragment •	function •	investigation •	justification
protein •	rehearsal •	shortage •	~~valley~~ •	veteran

1. Fog forms in the _____*valley*_____ at night.

2. The hospital issued a daily news _____ on the condition of the accident victims.

3. I found a _____ of glass on the floor when I was cleaning up.

4. He suffers from an _____ to heroin.

5. What was her _____ for doing that?

6. Unlike the US, Britain does not have a written _____.

7. The director insisted on having an extra _____ because some of the cast didn't know their lines.

8. He is a Vietnam War _____.

9. We were disappointed by the Senator's lack of _____.

10. A balanced budget is the most important _____ of the governor's plan.

11. There was a police _____ into the causes of the crash.

12. The foreign _____ attended the opening ceremony and made a speech.

13. Import controls have resulted in a _____ of spare parts.

14. What is the _____ of that red switch?

15. You need more _____ in your diet: you should eat more meat, eggs and fish.

Adjectives 1

Complete the sentences using the adjectives in the box. Use each adjective once only. The first one has been done for you as an example.

broad	•	contagious	•	~~desirable~~	• emotional
federal	•	genuine	•	intellectual	• loud
outrageous	•	relieved	•	sensible	• unclear

1. He lived in a highly _____*desirable*_____ part of Manhattan.

2. The statue was made from _____ Inca gold.

3. Because the instructions were _____, the student didn't know whether he was permitted to use a dictionary in the text.

4. He made an _____ appeal for funds for the charity.

5. After waiting for several hours, the parents were _____ to hear that their son was now in a stable condition.

6. The careers officer recommended that candidates wear smart and _____ clothes to their job interviews.

7. Turn down the radio – it's too _____.

8. The whole area was isolated because of the risk of spreading this highly _____ disease.

9. Having failed at the _____ court, he decided to take his case to the Supreme Court.

10. David was thought to be highly _____ whereas his brother was less academic.

11. Michelle's interests in music were very _____ – she had many different influences.

12. George's _____ behavior at the company outing almost cost him his job.

10

© Bloomsbury Publishing. For reference see *American English Study Dictionary* (1-901659-69-0)

Adjectives 2

Complete the sentences using the adjectives in the box. Use each adjective once only. The first one has been done for you as an example.

---

advanced • biased • critical • delighted • effective • energetic
favorable • ideal • ~~immediate~~ • judgmental • lasting
memorable • obvious • persistent • random • significant

---

1. He wasted no time in expressing his anger. He wrote an ___*immediate*___ letter of complaint.

2. You can see the sadness in his eyes. It is _____ that he is unhappy.

3. Our tutor is _____ toward the students in our class who like poetry – he always gives them good marks.

4. There was no logic or pattern to the attacks – they seem to be totally _____.

5. The professor of philosophy is very _____ – he is quick to say whether something is morally right or wrong – and he lets you know it!

6. This is the perfect beach – it's _____ for a barbecue or a game of volleyball.

7. I'll never forget the birth of our first child – it's probably the most _____ moment of my life so far.

8. The Vice-Principal unveiled the statue as a _____ memorial to his long-serving predecessor.

9. Of course I'm happy to have passed the exam. More than that, I'm _____.

10. It was very _____ that the professor didn't accept the award. He was expressing his disagreement with the central policies of the awarding body.

11. The technology used to make these new circuit boards is very _____ . We only use the most up-to-date techniques.

12. The rain put a stop to our baseball game. I hope the weather is more _____ for the big game tomorrow.

13. Henry would never give up until he got what he wanted – he was very _____.

14. Ice hockey is a very _____ sport. The best players are always on the move.

15. There are several ways to work more efficiently, but I find that prioritizing one's workload is the most _____ .

16. The newspaper report was highly _____ of the senator's conduct. It concluded that his behavior was unacceptable.

Verbs 1

Use the verbs in the box below to complete the sentences. The first question has been done for you as an example.

accuse • acknowledge • bear • benefit • classify • ~~decline~~ • exhaust launch • overcome • persuade • protect • regulate • relate • restore

1. Sales of jeans could _____ *decline* _____ this year due to the growing popularity of cargo pants.

2. The police must _____ all lines of enquiry before closing an unsolved case.

3. After months of painstaking work, they managed to _____ the car to its former glory.

4. The professor managed to _____ his nerves and give an excellent speech.

5. Many people think the tomato is a vegetable, whereas it is in fact correct to _____ it as a fruit.

6. Georgina was considering dropping out of college. Thankfully, her parents managed to _____ her to stay on for another year and then decide.

7. The tutor would _____ the late arrival of a student with a nod and a gesture to sit down.

8. The NYPD's mission is to _____ and serve the people of New York.

9. This lecture is incredibly boring! I don't think I can _____ it any longer!

10. If you don't acknowledge sources in your assignment, the examiner will _____ you of plagiarism.

11. Tom found it difficult to _____ to his brother – they didn't have much in common.

12. It is often tempting for governments to try to _____ areas of business, but it can be counterproductive to interfere with market forces.

13. Over the next few years, the US economy is set to _____ from a strong technology-driven economy.

14. Many companies use exhibitions as an opportunity to _____ a new product.

12

Verbs 2

The sentences in *Column A* contain examples of useful verbs. In *Column B* there are definitions of the verbs. Read the examples and match the verbs (in *italics*) with the definitions. Then write the infinitive forms into the spaces in the definitions in Column B. The first one has been done for you as an example.

Column A	Column B
1. The Governor was *accompanied* to the dinner by his wife.	a) _____ means to promise formally
2. The two professors *discussed* the theory on into the night.	b) _____ means to keep something safe
3. The clerk *handles* the majority of customers in the store.	c) _____*accompany*_____ means to go with
4. The price of textbooks has *increased* by 5% in the last decade.	d) _____ means to give someone a better job
5. As soon as he saw the crime, he *notified* the police.	e) _____ means to talk about a serious matter or problem
6. The President *pledged* to cut taxes by 2% in his first term of office.	f) _____ means to write a name officially in a list
7. The doctor *prescribed* a course of medication for the patient's ailment.	g) _____ means to pass a test or one section of a competition and so go on to the next stage
8. The assistant manager was *promoted* to a higher position in the company.	h) _____ means to deal with something
9. The building was *protected* by a high-security camera system.	i) _____ means to rise, grow or expand
10. The athlete *qualified* for the final round with a time of 4.46 minutes.	j) _____ means to know what something means
11. The student failed because she forgot to *register* for the exam.	k) _____ means to tell someone to use something (usually for their health)
12. The student didn't *understand* the complex equation.	l) _____ means to tell someone something formally

Verbs 3

The sentences in *Column A* contain examples of useful verbs. In *Column B* there are definitions of the verbs. Read the examples and match the verbs (in *italics*) with the definitions. Then write the infinitive forms into the spaces in the definitions in *Column B*. One has been done for you as an example.

Column A	Column B
1. She offered to help him in the kitchen and he *accepted*.	a) _____ means to say or write what someone or something is like
2. The company's share price was *boosted* by strong sales.	b) _____ means to use more of something than you need
3. After several complaints, the loud music finally *ceased* at two in the morning.	c) _____ means to try to make someone do something, especially something pleasant or wrong
4. The criminal was *described* as having red hair and wearing spectacles.	d) _____ means not to notice
5. The student was *encouraged* to apply to Harvard by his tutor.	e) _____ means to set free
6. In some states smoking has been *forbidden* in public spaces.	f) ___*accept*___ means to say 'yes' or agree to something
7. We turned off all the heating so as not to *waste* energy.	g) _____ means to divide or keep apart
8. She *overlooked* several errors when marking the students' papers.	h) _____ means to tell someone not to do something
9. After an hour of discussion he managed to *persuade* the client to buy his product.	i) _____ means to help someone to do something by giving them confidence
10. The animal was *released* back into the wild after three months.	j) _____ means to help to increase
11. The sales division is *separated* into two units: sales and marketing.	k) _____ means to get someone to do what you want by explaining or asking
12. She tried to *tempt* him with another piece of cake, but he declined.	l) _____ means to stop

Prepositions

The sentences in this exercise contain mistakes. The mistakes are all in the prepositions and there are three types:

1.   missing preposition   I spoke∧him about this last week.   *to*
2.   wrong preposition   We're meeting again in∧Tuesday.   *on*
3.   unnecessary preposition   I'll phone ~~to~~ you tomorrow.

Find the mistakes in the following sentences and correct them.

1.   The government is underwriting for the costs of the exhibition.

2.   He will sue you from libel.

3.   The company will meet to your expenses.

4.   I don't have my driver's license by me.

5.   Can I pay later, as I'm rather short for cash right now?

6.   They thought about flying here but decided to come in car.

7.   We put our house through the market last August.

8.   The table measures 2 feet 7 feet.

9.   It's from the law to drive in the dark without lights.

10.   She won at first prize in the art competition.

11.   We have received a letter our daughter.

12.   He wants to spend at more time with his family.

13.   Through the terms of the agreement, the goods should be delivered in October.

14.   There's only a thin wall from his office and mine, so I hear everything he says.

Cause & effect

Words such as *because*, *consequently* and *since* help to explain how one thing causes a change in another thing.

Exercise 1. Identify the expressions that show cause and effect in the following sentences and underline them. The first one has been done for you as an example.

1. The boy slowed down <u>so that</u> his grandmother could catch up.

2. I therefore have decided not to grant his request.

3. The game was canceled because of the rain.

4. It was snowing hard so we could not go for a walk.

5. The child was very excited, and consequently could not sleep.

6. She is only fifteen, and thus is not eligible for the over-sixteens competition.

7. We were late on account of the fog.

8. The dog is wet because he has been in the river.

9. Since she is ill, you cannot ask her to help you.

10. The traffic was bumper to bumper and, as a result, Josh missed his train.

11. I am sorry that owing to staff shortages, we cannot supply your order on time.

12. They had to run to the theater so as not to miss the performance.

Exercise 2. Write five sentences, each containing a different one of the cause and effect expressions identified in Exercise 1.

_____

_____

_____

_____

_____

_____

16

Contrast & comparison

This exercise will help you to review some of the expressions that are used in English to explain how two or more things are different or how they are similar.

Exercise 1. Write each of the following words or expressions in the correct column in the table below. The first two have been done for you as examples.

alike • although • as • correspondingly • different from
differ from • however • in common • in contrast to
instead • in the same way • just as • like
nevertheless • on the other hand • similarly • similar to • unlike

Contrast	Comparison
alike	although

Exercise 2. Choose the correct word or expression to complete each of these sentences.

1. The report was very short; _____ , it was filled with important information.

    (A) unlike   (B) nevertheless

2. He's _____ his mother in many ways, but has his father's good looks.

    (A) like   (B) alike

3. The movie is _____ good as the book.

    (A) just as   (B) in common

4. On the one hand, he's a good salesman, but _____ , he can't work out discounts correctly.

    (A) in the same way   (B) on the other hand

Explaining & adding more information

When you write your essay for the Test of Written English, you may want to give examples, emphasize certain points and add more information. Expressions such as *for instance, to clarify* and *moreover* will help you to do this.

Choose the correct word or expression to complete each of these sentences.

1. My boss is going on vacation next month, _____ she'll be away from the office for about four weeks.

   (A) in other words   (B) for instance

2. Green vegetables _____ cabbage and broccoli are my least favorite food.

   (A) as well as   (B) such as

3. He's a wildlife photographer and _____ writes articles for newspapers.

   (A) also   (B) similarly

4. English is the language spoken by the people of the USA, Canada, the UK, New Zealand and Australia. _____, English is one of the international languages of business.

   (A) In addition   (B) Like

5. I dislike only one subject in college, _____ French.

   (A) namely   (B) to clarify

6. We all felt cold, wet and hungry; _____, we were lost.

   (A) moreover   (B) for example

7. They have two vehicles _____ the pickup truck.

   (A) besides   (B) also

8. The kitchen is on the first floor, _____, the floor at street level.

   (A) furthermore   (B) that is

Don't forget to keep a record of the words and expressions that you have learned, review your notes from time to time and try to use new vocabulary items whenever possible.

© Bloomsbury Publishing. For reference see *American English Study Dictionary* (1-901659-69-0)

Identifying the task

In order to score highly in the Test of Written English, you must understand what the writing task is. Some of the words and phrases that you may see in the essay topic are grouped in Column A. Match the italicized words from Column A with their definitions in Column B. The first one has been done for you as an example.

Column A	Column B
Agreeing or disagreeing	1. _____ = give your reasons for something
Do you *agree* or *disagree* . . .?	
Do you *support* or *oppose* . . .?	2. _____ = to look at two things side by side to see how they are different
	3. _____ = in what way
Stating a preference	4. _____ = to have a different opinion
Compare…	
In your *opinion*, which is better?	5. _____ = to write what something is like
Which would you *prefer*?	
	6. _____ = to give something your approval or favor
	7. _____ = to make something different
Giving an explanation	8. _____ = what someone thinks about something
Describe…	
Explain…	9. _____ = to have the same opinion or to accept an idea
Why do you think…?	
	10. _____ = for what reason
	11. _____ = to be against something
Making an argument	
How…?	12. _____ = to like something better than something else
If you could *change* (something), what would you change?	

> Don't forget to keep a record of the words and expressions that you have learned, review your notes from time to time and try to use new vocabulary items whenever possible.

© Bloomsbury Publishing. For reference see *American English Study Dictionary* (1-901659-69-0)

Opinion, attitude and belief

Exercise 1. The words in bold in the following sentences are all used to talk about opinion and belief. However, the words are grammatically incorrect (for example, a noun has been used instead of an adjective, or a verb has been used instead of a noun, etc.) or sometimes a noun has been used which has the wrong meaning. Put the words into their correct form.

1. In my **opinionated**, technology is moving too quickly.

2. As far as I am **concerning**, happiness is more important than money.

3. Scientists are **convincingly** that human degradation of the environment is causing thousands of species to become extinct.

4. The government are **regardless** the Third World debt as a major problem to global economic development.

5. Hundreds of people called the television station to register their **disapprove** of the presenter's behaviour.

6. She **maintenance** that most young people would rather work than go to school.

7. Do you **reckoning** that there will be an election in the next two years?

8. We strongly **suspicion** that the proposal to develop the computer facilities will not go ahead.

9. I **doubtful** that the new government will keep all its promises.

10. Do you **disapproval** of smoking?

11. I take strong **except** to people coming late or cancelling appointments at short notice.

12. A lot of people are **fanatic** about sport in general and football in particular.

13. American health inspectors are **obsession** about cleanliness in restaurant kitchens.

14. After years of struggle, the **moderations** have gained control of the party.

15. He has very **conservatism** views and disapproves of change.

16. The government are **commitment** to the struggle to end institutional racism in the police force.

17. She was **dedication** to her family and would do anything to protect them.

18. They come from a strongly **tradition** family who still believe in arranged marriages.

Exercise 2. Decide if these nouns and adjectives refer to (1) political beliefs or (2) personal convictions and philosophies. Can you think of any other words or expressions that you could add?

> opinionated • a republican • pragmatic • a Muslim • an intellectual
> a revolutionary • tolerant • a moralist • narrow-minded
> bigoted • open-minded • a vegan • left-wing • right-wing • a socialist
> a royalist • a Buddhist • a conservative • a liberal • a communist
> a vegetarian • dogmatic • moral • a fascist
> religious • a Hindu • middle-of-the-road • an anarchist • a stoic

Exercise 1. Use the time clauses in the boxes to complete the sentences. Pay particular attention to the words that come before or after the time clause.

Part 1: One action or situation occurring before another action or situation

prior to • previously • earlier • formerly • precede • by the time

1.   ....the advent of the Industrial Revolution, pollution was virtually unheard of.

2.   ....the army had restored order, the city had been almost completely devastated.

3.   ....known as Burma, the republic of Myanmar is undergoing a slow and painful political transformation.

4.   A sudden drop in temperature will usually ....a blizzard.

5.   It was my first trip on an aeroplane.   ....I'd always gone by train.

6.   The President made a speech praising charity organizations working in Mozambique. ....that day he had promised massive economic aid to stricken areas.

Part 2: One action or situation occurring at the same time as another action or situation

while / as / just as • during / throughout • at that very moment • in the meantime / meanwhile

1.   ....the senator was making his speech, thousands of demonstrators took to the streets.

2.   .... the speech they jeered and shouted slogans.

3.   The senator continued speaking.   .... the police were ordered onto the streets.

4.   He finished the speech with a word of praise for the police.   .... the sun came out and shone down on the angry demonstrators.

Part 3: One action or situation occurring after another action or situation

afterwards • as soon as / once / the minute that • following

1.   .... the earthquake, emergency organizations around the world swung into action.

2.   .... the stock market collapsed, there was panic buying on an unprecedented scale.

3.   The Klondike gold rush lasted from 1896 to 1910.   .... the area became practically deserted overnight.

Exercise 2. Look at these words and expressions and decide if we usually use them to talk about (1) the past, (2) the past leading to the present, (3) the present or (4) the future. Try to write a sentence for each one.

for the next few weeks • as things stand • ever since • in medieval times one day • nowadays • from now on • back in the 1990s over the past six weeks • over the coming weeks and months in another five years' time • in those days • a few decades ago lately • at this moment in time • at the turn of the century in my childhood / youth • at this point in history • by the end of this year for the foreseeable future • for the past few months • last century these days • from 1996 to 1998 • sooner or later

Phrasal verbs 1

Phrasal verbs are very common in English, and should be learnt like any other item of English vocabulary. In the TOEFL®, they are tested in the Listening Comprehension section, and appear frequently in other parts of the test.

The exercises in this book look at some of the most commonly-used phrasal verbs.

Complete the following phrasal verbs with a preposition(s) or particle(s) from the box. The meaning of the phrasal verb is given in parentheses at the end of each sentence.

over • back • into • forward • of • on
down • to • up • behind • out • in • off • with

1.   Some parents are criticized for the way they **bring** _____ their children. *(raise)*

2.   The committee members **fell** _____ over plans for the new health centre. *(argued)*

3.   They refused to **face** _____ _____ their responsibilities, with disastrous consequences. *(accept an unpleasant state of affairs, and try to deal with it)*

4.   The President decided to **call** _____ his visit to Europe. *(not to go ahead with something)*

5.   It is only at election time that senators **count** _____ support from their constituents. *(rely / depend)*

6.   Many developing countries are failing to **catch** _____ _____ their more developed neighbours. *(get to the same level)*

7.   It can take months or even years for political scandals to **die** _____. *(become less strong)*

8.   An alarming number of students **drop** _____ _____ school early every year. *(leave)*

9.   Major international companies can't **figure** _____ the popularity of the anticapitalist movement. *(find it hard to understand)*

10.   If they examined the issues more closely, they would **find** _____ the reasons. *(discover)*

11.   As we **grow** _____ our priorities change. *(change from being children to being adults),*

12.   Students can be quite creative with the reasons they give for not **handing** _____ their homework. *(giving your homework to your teachers)*

13.   Salaries very rarely **keep** _____ _____ the cost of living. *(rise at the same speed as)*

14.   The latest Avicenna report **leaves** _____ the reasons for demographic shifts. *(does not include)*

15.   It does **point** _____ the mistakes made by the agency over the last few years. *(show)*

16.   Before you write your essay, you should **look** _____ the Party's history. *(research)*

17.   Many employees **carried** _____ working despite pressure from the unions. *(continued)*

18.   Once people **fall** _____ with their mortgage payments, they come under extreme financial pressure from their bank. *(become late)*

19.   The first step to a healthier lifestyle is to **cut** _____ _____ the number of cigarettes you smoke each day. *(reduce)*

20.   It is becoming more common for people to **cut** _____ meat from their diet. *(stop eating)*

21.   During the 1990's, a lot of state-run hospitals were **taken** _____ by private trusts. *(start to do something in place of someone else)*

22.   When computer technology fails us, we have to **make do** _____ more primitive methods. They're called 'pen and paper'. *(use something because there is nothing else available)*

23.   In this essay, I'd like to **put** _____ the arguments in favour of global capitalism. *(suggest or state the case for something)*

24.   When I **look** _____ _____ my childhood, I remember the many sacrifices my parents made for me. *(think about something that happened in the past)*

Also see: **Phrasal verbs 2 - 5**
            Idioms and colloquialisms 1 - 5

Don't forget to keep a written record of all the new phrasal verbs you learn, and try to use them whenever possible so that they become a part of your 'active' vocabulary.

Complete the second sentence in each pair with a phrasal verb from the box so that it has the same meaning as the first sentence. You will need to change the verb form in most of the sentences.

| break down • carry out • cut back on • cut off • do away with |
| do up • end up • fall through • hold up • keep on • let down |
| let off • pull out • pull through • show up • sort out |
| split up • wear off • wear out • work out |

1. Peace talks between the two countries collapsed when neither side reached an agreement.
    Peace talks between the two countries _____ when neither side reached an agreement.

2. I'm trying to calculate if we've sold more this year than last year.
    I'm trying to _____ if we've sold more this year than last year.

3. The effects of the drug disappear after a few hours.
    The effects of the drug _____ after a few hours.

4. A lot of people exhaust themselves through overwork.
    A lot of people _____ themselves _____ through overwork.

5. Despite the severity of the disease, many people recover with the help of appropriate drugs.
    Despite the severity of the disease, many people _____ with the help of appropriate drugs.

6. Through careful negotiation, they were able to resolve the problem.
    Through careful negotiation, they were able to _____ the problem.

7. When parents start to live apart, it can be particularly difficult for their children to cope.
    When parents _____ , it can be particularly difficult for their children to cope.

8. At the opening night, only a few audience members came.
    At the opening night, only a few audience members _____ .

9. The Australian partners stopped being a part of the deal at the last moment.
    The Australian partners _____ of the deal at the last moment.

10. People celebrate the Chinese New Year by exploding fireworks in the street.
    People celebrate the Chinese New Year by _____ fireworks in the street.

11. It is pointless relying on people to help you if they don't do as they promised.
    It is pointless relying on people to help you if they _____ you _____ .

Phrasal verbs 2

12. New government pension plans mean that many people will continue working well into their seventies.

   New government pension plans mean that many people will _____ working well into their seventies.

13. The planned changes were delayed because committee members argued among themselves.

   The planned changes were _____ because committee members argued among themselves.

14. At the last minute, the plans for the proposed freeway didn't take place.

   At the last minute, the plans for the proposed freeway _____.

15. During the recession, many workers in the primary sector became jobless.

   During the recession, many workers in the primary sector _____ jobless.

16. Doctors did some tests on the patients.

   Doctors _____ some tests on the patients.

17. Minor economies, such as spending less on staff costs, can often prevent a company sliding into bankruptcy.

   Minor economies, such as _____ staff costs, can often prevent a company sliding into bankruptcy.

18. We were accidentally disconnected in the middle of our phone call.

   We were accidentally _____ in the middle of our phone call.

19. Once the government removed quotas, the market was flooded with cheap foreign imports.

   Once the government _____ quotas, the market was flooded with cheap foreign imports.

20. It cost almost $8 million to renovate the stadium, by which time the team was in serious financial difficulties.

   It cost almost $8 million to _____ the stadium, by which time the team was in serious financial difficulties.

Also see: **Phrasal verbs 1, 3, 4, 5**

   Idioms and colloquialisms 1 - 5

These sentences can all be completed with a phrasal verb using *come* or *get*. In one case, either may be possible. Make sure you use the correct form of the verb in each one.

1. In rural districts, it can be difficult to _____ **by** without a car.

2. Scientists _____ **across** the cure by accident, while studying the health benefits of a rare species of plant.

3. The anti-smoking message is finally _____ **through** to people.

4. Large industries can no longer _____ **away** with dumping industrial waste in rivers.

5. Doctors realised there was going to be a problem when several people in the same town _____ **down** with suspected food poisoning.

6. It can be very difficult to _____ **down** to studying for exams when the weather is nice.

7. It was only after he _____ **into** his inheritance after his father died that he was able to expand the company.

8. After the revolution, it took almost five years for the country to _____ **round** to opening its borders.

9. The governor _____ **up** against a lot of opposition from locals when she proposed building a jail near the city limits.

10. Developed countries are usually able to _____ **through** a period of recession by drawing on financial reserves.

11. There was strong resistance to the union when it urged workers to _____ **out** on strike.

12. People who live in close proximity to one another must learn to _____ **on** with their neighbors.

13. Nothing _____ **of** the company's plans to develop solar-powered vehicles.

14. The final bill for the project _____ **to** almost $10 million.

15. For most poor people, _____**out** of the cycle of poverty can be next to impossible.

16. In any dispute with an insurance company, it is usually the consumer who _____ **off** the worst.

17. When supply of a particular good exceeds demand, it is common for the price to _____ **down**.

18. By the time the message _____ **through** it was too late to evacuate the residents.

19. The country never _____ **over** the effects of the civil war.

20. Generally, people are reluctant to break rules, but will try to _____ **round** them somehow.

Also see: **Phrasal verbs 1, 2, 4, 5**
Idioms and colloquialisms 1 - 5

25

Phrasal verbs 4

The following sentences all use phrasal verbs with *give*, *go* or *look*. However, half of them use the wrong phrasal verb. Decide which ones are wrong and replace them with the correct phrasal verb, which you will find in the other sentences.

1.   I'd like you to **look after** these figures and tell me if you think the project is possible.

2.   As ticket prices **go up**, fewer people go to the theater and prefer to stay at home with a video.

3.   People who have to **give in** older relatives or other dependants should receive financial support.

4.   The government had decided to stand firm on their decision, but under pressure from protesters, they decided to **go into** and reduce tax on petrol.

5.   The committee were asked to **look into** the latest crime statistics and try to establish a pattern.

6.   It is important not to let the fire **go out**, as it's the main source of power.

7.   Very few children **give off** their end-of-year school exams.

8.   The threat of severe reprisals meant that many refused to **give** themselves **up** to the police.

9.   Before entering an agreement, it is essential to **go off** the details very carefully.

10. People who want to know how to **go about** starting their own company should talk to a trained adviser.

11. Some people tend to **go over** others who are less fortunate purely because of their financial situation.

12. There were very few clues to the crime, and police didn't have enough information to **go on**.

13. People often **look over** the idea of starting their own company when they realise the risks that are involved.

14. Even if you fail the first time, you should **go on** trying.

15. After years of decline, government investment is revitalizing the area, and things are beginning to **look up**.

16. The first step to a healthier lifestyle is to **give up** smoking.

17. New legislation lays down strict penalties for factories which **look up to** poisonous fumes.

18. We decided not to **go through** with our plans until we had sufficient capital.

19. Although children should **look forward to** their parents, many rebel against their values and way of life.

20. We asked them for more information, but they refused to **look down on** details.

Also see: **Phrasal verbs 1,2, 3, 5**

                  Idioms and colloquialisms 1 - 5

Phrasal verbs 5

The verbs and particles in the two boxes can be combined to make phrasal verbs, which can then be used to complete the sentences below.

Decide which phrasal verbs go into each sentence, and write the answers in the crossword grid. In many cases, you will need to change the form of the verb (eg, past participle, infinitive, third person 's', etc). The meaning of each phrasal verb is in italics at the end of each sentence.

Don't forget that some phrasal verbs need two particles.

| talk • put • take • run • turn |
| opt • stand • pick • make • set |

| on • off • with • for • around • against |
| down • aside • in • out • up • after |

Clues across (➜)

1. Accommodations in some cities are so expensive that some people cannot even afford to _____ the eight weeks' deposit that is required. *(to make a deposit)* **Answer = put down**

4. They were reluctant to make changes, but we managed to _____ them _____. *(to persuade somebody)*

5. Children often _____ one of their parents, either in their mannerisms or in the way they look. *(to resemble)*

6. After _____ a few unexpected difficulties, they decided to scrap the project. *(to stop because something is in the way)*

8. They were _____ of the apartment by their landlord when they could no longer afford the rent, and ended up living on the street. *(to be forced to leave)*

11. When I was at school, some teachers unfairly _____ children who disliked sports and preferred more creative interests and pastimes. *(to choose someone to attack or criticize)*

12. Although many companies offer their employees a pension plan, many decide to _____ of the program and make their own arrangements. *(to decide not to take part in something)*

16. A lot of applicants expressed an interest in the job, but only a handful _____ for the interview. *(to arrive for a meeting, appointment, etc)*

19. Air pollution can _____ asthma and other chest diseases in those most vulnerable. *(to start)*

20. People who use credit cards unwisely can easily _____ debts of thousands of dollars every month. *(to make debts go up quickly)*

21. By the time he was 18, he had _____ his mind that he wanted to be famous. *(to decide on something)*

Clues down (↓)

1. It's often a good idea to _____ some money for a 'rainy day'. *(to save money)*

2. Technology is moving at such a fast pace it is no longer possible to _____ all the latest developments. *(to understand or assimilate information)*

3. Nobody was _____ by the government's false figures on unemployment. *(to be fooled or tricked)*

5. He _____ the job that was offered to him, even though he was desperate for the money. *(to refuse something which is offered)*

Phrasal verbs 5

7. Most people will _____ a stressful job if the money is good enough. *(to tolerate something which is not very pleasant)*

9. He was unable to make the speech, so I was asked to _____ and make it on his behalf. *(to take the place of someone - often also used with 'for')*

10. A lot of people are _____ the idea of working for themselves because of the lack of a regular salary. *(to be discouraged from doing something, usually because of a potentially negative outcome)*

13. Once bad weather _____, people tend to stay at home rather than go out. *(to start and become permanent)*

14. Doctors and medical experts were unable to _____ why some people survived the virus and others didn't. *(to understand or know the reason for something)*

15. She _____ a story about ghosts in the cellar to stop us going down there, but of course we didn't believe her. *(to invent a story)*

17. At the age of 38 he _____ the post of President, but lacked sufficient experience to be taken seriously. *(to apply for a job in politics, competing against other people for the same job)*

18. Despite massive promotion by the tourist board it took a long time for tourism to _____ again after the terrorist attacks. *(to improve, to get better)*

Also see: Phrasal verbs 1 - 4

Idioms and colloquialisms 1 - 5

Words with similar meanings are tested in the TOEFL® Reading Comprehension. It is also useful to know alternatives to other words to make your writing more varied, and to improve your general reading skills.

Choose a word from the box that is closest in meaning to the words / expressions in bold in the sentences, and use these to complete the crossword.

albeit • abrupt • absurd • baffle • caliber • coarse • convey • demand
detect • elicit • enrich • finite • forbid • handle • hasten • launch
mirror • narrow • notion • oblige • obtain • placid • potent • prompt • relate
reveal • robust • settle • steady • submit • unique • varied

Clues across (→)

1. The threat of major repercussions failed to **induce** the governor to act.

3. In the summer, the weather on the east coast can be pleasant **though** changeable.

4. The USA and Cuba have often tried to **resolve** their differences, but with little effect.

5. He was asked to **disclose** government secrets in exchange for money.

6. We were able to **notice** a hint of optimism in her latest report.

11. The **constant and continuous** rise in unemployment has been counteracted by a drop in inflation.

12. He thought that the work was beneath a person of his **intellect and ability**.

16. They were unable to **get** any useful information from the directors.

17. The governor was asked to **insist on** new measures to combat crime.

18. His inability to act quickly enough will probably **accelerate** their decision to fire him.

19. The department was asked to **propose** some ideas for increasing their share of the market.

20. His plans seem to **confuse** most people he presents them to.

22. He spoke with a **powerful** mixture of threats and promises.

24. The organization hopes to **start** a new program of reforms.

25. Some crops, such as beans, **benefit** the soil in which they are planted.

26. The senator's relaxed attitude to the problem didn't **reflect** those of his constituents.

27. The country has a **strong and vigorous** economy that has helped it to survive several financial crises.

28. It is **ridiculous** to believe that industry doesn't harm the environment.

Clues down (↓)

2. It took him some time to **tell** the story, and it was late when he eventually finished.

3. The committee's **sudden** change of plan surprised everyone.

© Bloomsbury Publishing. For reference see *American English Study Dictionary* (1-901659-69-0)

Similar meanings 1

7. We were unable to **obtain** any information from the committee.

8. There was general approval when the announcement to **ban** smoking was made.

9. The arts festival comprised a **diverse** program of events.

10. The world's coal resources are **limited** and are forecast to run out soon.

13. She asked us to **give** her best wishes to the chairperson.

14. The final product has a **rough** surface which can cause cuts or grazes.

15. The government won the election by a very **small** majority.

16. The college rules **require** all students to refrain from smoking and drinking.

18. He was asked to **deal with** the situation with tact and discretion.

21. The vegetation on the island is **extremely rare**.

22. The normally **calm** nature of the town was interrupted by the arrival of a TV crew.

23. The **idea** that politics and religion should work together wasn't appreciated by everyone.

Similar meanings 2

Rearrange the bold letters at the end of each sentence to form words that are similar in meaning to the underlined words / expressions in each sentence. The last letter of each word is the first letter of the next word. The first and last ones have been done for you.

assert
conventional

1. If you want people to take you seriously, you should <u>state firmly</u> your reasons for change. **satser**

2. Until the government introduces stricter laws, industries will continue to pump <u>poisonous</u> gases into the atmosphere. **oxcti**

3. The machine was designed to <u>grind</u> rocks to dust for industrial purposes. **uschr**

4. The TV campaign helped to <u>increase</u> public awareness of the drug problem. **eghnhite**

5. There was a <u>small</u> charge for membership of the organization, but the advantages of joining were substantial. **aninlom**

6. There was no chance of an <u>enduring</u> peace between the two countries owing to political differences. **tgnlsia**

7. Before you speak, <u>collect</u> your thoughts and decide exactly what you are going to say. **aghrte**

8. The laws in the country are so <u>inflexible</u> that nobody dares break them for fear of serious punishment. **digri**

9. Environmentalists predict an <u>extreme</u> rise in sea levels over the next hundred years. **imadrcat**

10. The Vice President has tremendous <u>personal appeal</u> and charm. **shacraim**

11. Orhan Pamuk received great <u>praise</u> for his novel 'My Name is Red' **micacla**

12. The cheapest <u>method</u> of traveling around the USA is by Greyhound bus. **amsne**

13. The book offered a very <u>superficial</u> overview of a serious scientific subject. **aswhlol**

14. During the election, the Republicans made a great effort to <u>attract</u> younger voters. **owo**

15. There was surprisingly little <u>resistance</u> to the government's plans for compulsory identity cards. **popinoosti**

16. Doctors were perplexed to discover that in most cases, any benefits the drug may have had were <u>minimal</u>. **gebglieiln**

17. His policies on economic reform were <u>inconsistent</u>, and he lost credibility and support as a result. **ctraeir**

18. When <u>ordinary</u> medicines fail to work, many patients turn to alternative cures such as homeopathy. **nontvclenioa**

Similar meanings 3

Look at sentences 1 - 14 and choose a word from the box that has a similar meaning to the words and expressions in bold. Write these words in the grid. The first one has been done as an example.

If you do it correctly, you will reveal a word in the shaded vertical strip that is a synonym of the word '**typical**' in this sentence:

The strong sense of community is __typical__ of an area where people feel they are an underclass who must struggle to survive.

adequate • advantage • comprehensive • contemporary • crucial exemplifies • hazardous • indispensable • inventive • resolute rudimentary • survey • tenacious • thriving

1. **Modern** art is often criticized as being pretentious and sensationalist.
2. Environmentalists have proven that living in industrial areas can be **dangerous** for your health.
3. Knowledge of two or more foreign languages is a distinct **benefit** in many jobs.
4. They made a **determined** effort to re-establish cultural and diplomatic ties.
5. There is criticism that unemployment benefits are barely **enough** to support some families.
6. It was **extremely important** that the press respected the privacy of the President's family during such a difficult period.
7. Until natural resources were exhausted, the town was a **flourishing** community of almost 2000 people.
8. The new building **symbolizes** modern American architecture at its best.
9. Most people's knowledge of a foreign language barely extends beyond the most **basic**.
10. Water is **vital** for survival; without it, there would be no life.
11. The **opinion poll** taken before the election did not reflect the final result.
12. He was a **resilient** man who believed in fighting for his principles.
13. The company came up with some **innovative** ideas, most of which were commercially successful.
14. **Extensive** knowledge of a country's history is not necessary in order to appreciate its culture.

	First Letter	Rest of word
1	c	ontemporary
2		
3		
4		
5		
6		
7		
8		
9		
10		
11		
12		
13		
14		

Choose a word from the box that is closest in meaning to the words / expressions in bold in the sentences, and use these to complete the crossword.

---

account • acquire • broaden • clarify • curious • decline • dictate
diverse • dormant • endorse • exhaust • fallacy • fertile • forfeit • infancy
involve • overtly • portray • promote • recover • replace • suspect • tedious
triumph • uniform • unravel • vibrant • visibly

Clues across (→)

3. To increase profits, many retail outlets **substitute** shop assistants for machines that can take their customer's spending money.

5. They were **noticeably** upset by the events that had taken place.

7. People who have **boring** jobs are rarely very productive.

8. They were unable to **support** my application for a transfer to another department.

10. The company **openly** flouted the regulations regarding emissions of poisonous gases.

11. Not enough steps are being taken to find alternate sources of power for when we eventually **use up** our supply of natural resources.

13. Most consumers want vegetables of the **same size** and color.

14. No one has ever been able to **solve** the mystery of her disappearance.

18. He was asked to **explain clearly** his plans for the project.

20. Along the river valley, the soil is very **rich**.

22. It can take a lot of time and effort to **obtain** a green card.

23. There has been a sharp **drop** in the number of people going to college.

24. If you want to **reclaim** the money you have lost, you will have to fill in a claims form.

25. His early music was an **odd** mix of reggae and heavy metal.

26. The media likes to **depict** him as a national hero, when in fact he is little more than a criminal.

Similar meanings 4

Choose a word from the box that is closest in meaning to the words / expressions in bold in the sentences, and use these to complete the crossword.

---

account • acquire • broaden • clarify • curious • decline • dictate
diverse • dormant • endorse • exhaust • fallacy • fertile • forfeit • infancy
involve • overtly • portray • promote • recover • replace • suspect • tedious
triumph • uniform • unravel • vibrant • visibly

Clues down (↓)

1. In 1910, the aircraft industry was still in its **early stages of development**.

2. The aim of the organization is to **encourage** travel among young people.

4. They gave us their own **story** of what happened that night.

6. Travel can **increase** your knowledge of the world around you.

7. They scored a **victory** in their game against Mexico.

9. Volcanoes can remain **inactive** for years before erupting with very little warning.

12. We want to **include** the local community in our plans for a new shopping mall.

15. Until the economic recession, the town had a large and **lively** community.

16. Large, powerful countries should not feel they have the right to **tell** other countries what they can and cannot do.

17. If you fail to attend classes, you will **lose** your right to continue studying at the college.

19. Their first concert was a **varied** mix of classical and popular music.

20. It's a common **mistake** to assume that overseas companies are less efficient than our own ones.

21. We **think** it's going to be more difficult than we had originally hoped.

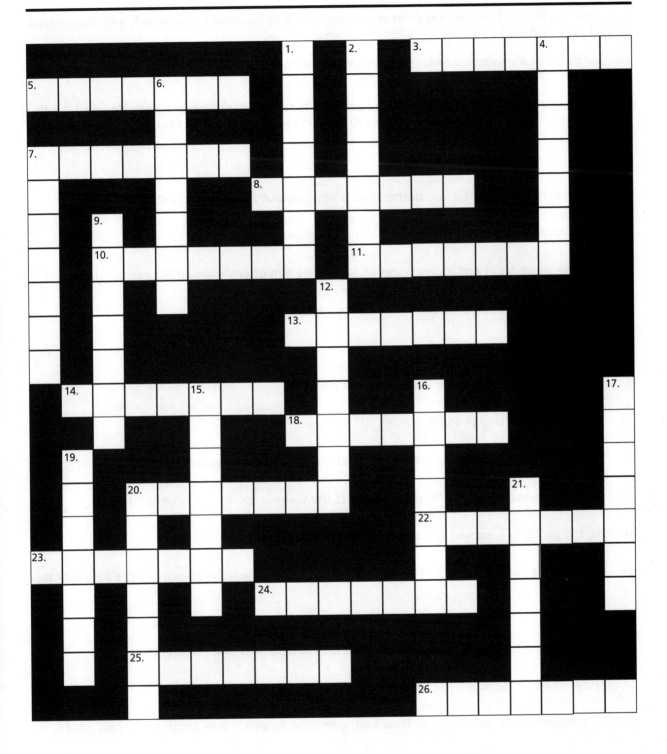

Similar meanings 5

Find words in the grid on the next page which are closest in meaning to the words and expressions in bold in sentences 1 - 26.

The words are in alphabetical order (the answer to number 1 begins with A, the answer to number 2 begins with B, and so on).

To find the words, you will need to read horizontally to the right (➜) and vertically down (↓) only. The number of letters in each word is given in brackets at the end of the sentence.

1.   I'm afraid your request is not **permissible** unless you put it in writing first. (10)

2.   You should give a **sensible** view of the current situation. (8)

3.   The **preservation** of endangered species is just one aim of environmental pressure groups. (12)

4.   The **protest** spread to all areas of the city by nightfall. (13)

5.   It was an **outstanding** performance which won her critical acclaim worldwide. (11)

6.   A lot of governments abuse **basic** human rights. (11)

7.   Wind can be used to **produce** power. (8)

8.   The two reports **illustrate** the problems that many inner-city dwellers face. (9)

9.   A change in the economic climate can **affect** the way we spend our earnings. (9)

10. All the protestors wanted was **fair legal treatment**. (7)

11. He earned a lot of professional **respect** by writing a well-researched report on the future of the

     market. (5)

12. He couldn't give a **valid** reason for his failure to comply with the rules. (10)

13. They did not understand the **importance** of the task that lay ahead. (9)

14. The project cost a lot of money. **However**, everyone agreed it was worth every cent. (12)

15. Many of the clothes at fashion shows are too **strange** for most people to wear. (10)

16. The changes were so slight that they were almost impossible to **see** with the naked eye. (8)

17. It's difficult to **measure** the value of the work he does for the college. (8)

18. Before they went any further, they had to get the **necessary** government permits. (9)

19. The system is **rather** old-fashioned and needs updating as soon as possible. (8)

20. The company carried out **detailed** research into the benefits of opening an office in Europe. (8)

21. The union delivered a final **demand** to the management. (9)

22. In the battle of the sexes, there can never be a true **winner**. (6)

23. There was **extensive** flooding which destroyed huge areas of crops. (10)

24. He was intensely **nationalistic**, and this was reflected in his policies. (9)

25. Their researches failed to **produce** the information they were looking for. (5)

26. The empire reached its **peak** at the beginning of the 19th century. (6)

Q	W	W	E	R	T	Y	U	I	O	O	U	T	L	A	N	D	I	S	H	P
A	I	N	F	L	U	E	N	C	E	S	D	F	E	G	H	J	K	L	Z	X
C	D	V	B	N	M	Q	W	E	R	T	M	A	G	N	I	T	U	D	E	Y
G	E	N	E	R	A	T	E	U	I	O	P	A	I	S	D	F	G	H	J	K
L	S	Z	X	C	V	B	N	E	X	C	E	P	T	I	O	N	A	L	M	Q
Q	P	W	Y	E	R	T	Y	U	I	O	O	P	I	A	S	D	F	G	H	P
J	R	K	I	L	Z	X	C	V	B	N	M	Q	M	W	E	H	R	T	Y	E
N	E	V	E	R	T	H	E	L	E	S	S	U	A	I	V	I	C	T	O	R
O	A	P	L	A	S	D	F	G	H	E	J	K	T	L	Z	G	X	C	V	C
B	D	N	D	M	T	R	E	W	O	R	I	Q	E	W	E	H	R	T	Y	E
U	I	O	P	A	S	D	F	G	H	V	J	K	L	Z	X	L	C	V	B	I
N	F	U	N	D	A	M	E	N	T	A	L	M	Z	E	N	I	T	H	Q	V
W	E	R	T	Y	C	U	I	O	P	T	A	S	D	F	G	G	H	J	K	E
J	U	S	T	I	C	E	U	L	T	I	M	A	T	U	M	H	Q	S	W	E
R	T	Y	U	I	E	O	D	E	M	O	N	S	T	R	A	T	I	O	N	P
A	S	K	D	F	P	G	H	J	K	N	L	Z	X	C	V	B	N	M	M	Q
Q	Q	U	A	N	T	I	F	Y	W	E	R	B	A	L	A	N	C	E	D	T
Y	U	D	I	O	A	P	R	E	Q	U	I	S	I	T	E	A	S	W	D	F
G	H	O	J	K	B	L	Z	X	C	V	T	H	O	R	O	U	G	H	B	N
M	Q	S	W	E	L	R	T	Y	U	I	O	P	A	S	D	F	G	A	H	J
K	L	Z	X	X	E	N	O	P	H	O	B	I	C	C	V	B	N	T	M	Q

Opposites 2

Replace the words in bold in these sentences with a word from the box which has an opposite meaning.

Verbs

withdrew •	fell •	rewarded •	loosened •	refused (to let) •	set
denied •	deteriorated •	abandoned •	forbade •	lowered
demolished •	retreated •	simplified •	attacked •	rejected

1. They **accepted** the offer of a ceasefire.
2. He **admitted** telling lies in his original statement.
3. The army slowly **advanced**, leaving a trail of devastation in its path.
4. They **agreed** to meet to discuss the future of the organization.
5. The senator **defended** his opponent's policies in a televised speech.
6. The apartments blocks they **built** were the ugliest in the city.
7. He **complicated** matters by rewriting the original proposal.
8. They **continued** their plans to assassinate the king when he opened Parliament.
9. He **deposited** $10,000 - half his college fees for the forthcoming year.
10. Relations between the two countries have **improved** considerably in the last year.
11. He **permitted** us to present our petition directly to the President.
12. The members of the gang were **punished** for their part in the riot.
13. He **raised** the overall standards of the company within two months of his appointment.
14. As soon as the sun **rose**, the demonstrators began to appear on the streets.
15. Prices **rose** sharply in the first three months of the fiscal year.
16. As soon as he had **tightened** the knots, he pushed the boat out.

Adjectives

scarce •	easy •	approximate •	dim •	compulsory
delicate •	innocent •	detrimental •	reluctant •	crude
even •	clear •	graceful •	considerable •	flexible

1. The meaning of his words was very **ambiguous**.
2. According to his colleagues, he's a very **awkward** person to deal with.
3. When she first started dancing, she was very **awkward**.
4. His policies were **beneficial** to the economy as a whole.
5. We need **exact** figures before we embark on a new venture.
6. The jury decided he was **guilty** of the crime.
7. Add up all the **odd** numbers between 1 and 20 to get a result.
8. Despite the weather, supplies of food after the harvest were **plentiful**.
9. The laws restricting pollution in the city are very **rigid**.
10. There is a **slight** difference in the way the company is run these days compared with a few years ago.
11. The device is very **sophisticated** and should only be operated by someone who is familiar with it.
12. The spices used in the production of some international dishes have a very **strong** flavour.
13. The **bright** light from the flashlight picked out details on the walls of the cave.
14. Attendance at afternoon classes should be **voluntary**.
15. A lot of students are **willing** to attend classes on Saturday morning.

Confusing words and false friends

<u>Confusing words</u> are two or more words which have a similar meaning to each other but are used in a different way.

Or

Are related to the same topic, but have a different meaning.

Or

Look similar, but have a different meaning.

<u>False friends</u> are words in English which have a similar-looking word in another language but which have a different meaning.

Complete the following sentences with the appropriate word.

1.　　**action / activity**
The police took immediate _____ when they realized the situation was getting out of hand.
Economic _____ stagnated as the recession took hold.

2.　　**advice / advise**
Can you _____ me on the best course of action to take?
He offered me some excellent _____ .

3.　　**affect / effect**
Cuts in spending will have a serious _____ on the health services.
The strike will seriously _____ train services.

4.　　**appreciable / appreciative**
There is an _____ difference between manslaughter and murder.
She was very _____ of our efforts to help.

5.　　**assumption / presumption**
They raised taxes on the _____ that it would help control spending.
It's sheer _____ for the government to suggest things have improved since they came to power.

6.　　**avoid / prevent**
Rapid government reforms managed to _____ a revolution taking place.
He's always trying to _____ taking a decision if he can help it.

7.　　**beside / besides**
The office is just _____ the bus station.
_____ their regular daytime job, many people do extra work in the evening.

8.　　**briefly / shortly**
_____ before the conflict began, the army pulled down the border posts.
The candidate spoke _____ about the need for political reform.

9.　　**channel / canal**
The television _____ received a formal complaint about the program.
The Panama _____ was built in the second half of the nineteenth century.

Confusing words and false friends

10.   conscientious / conscious
Most people are _____ of the need to protect the environment.
_____ workers should be rewarded for their hard work.

11.   continual / continuous
A _____ trade embargo has badly affected the economic infrastructure.
The computer has given us _____ problems ever since we installed it.

12.   control / inspect
Environmental health officers regularly _____ kitchens and other food preparation areas.
The government plans to _____ the price of meat to make sure it doesn't go up too much.

13.   criticism(s) / objection(s)
They didn't raise any _____ when we insisted on inspecting the figures.
The government's plan was met with severe _____ .

14.   damage / injury / harm
It was a severe _____ which needed immediate hospital treatment.
A lot of _____ was caused to buildings along the coast during the storm.
There's no _____ in taking a break from your job now and then.

15.   discover / invent
When did he _____ the telephone?
Did Alexander Fleming _____ penicillin?

16.   during / for / while
Shops were closed _____ the duration of the conflict.
_____ the transition from a dictatorship to democracy, the country experienced severe strikes and riots.
The bomb went off _____ the rebel leader was making his speech.

17.   however / moreover
The plan was good in theory. _____, in practice it was extremely difficult to implement.
The plan was excellent. _____, it was clear from the beginning that it was going to be a success.

18.   inconsiderate / inconsiderable
An _____ amount of money was wasted.
_____ behaviour makes life unpleasant for everybody.

19.   intolerable / intolerant
I consider his behaviour to be quite _____ .
The government is _____ of other political parties.

20.   job / work
Everybody has the right to a decent _____ with good pay.
Following the recession, many people are still looking for _____ .

21.   lay(s) / lie(s)

The city of Quito _____ near the equator.

The manager made it clear he intended to _____ down some strict rules.

22.   look at / watch

We must _____ the situation in Lugumba carefully, and be prepared to act if violence flares again.

We need to _____ the problem carefully and decide if there is anything we can do about it.

23.   permission / permit

I'm afraid we can't _____ photography in here.

They received _____ to attend the sessions as long as they didn't interrupt.

24.   possibility / chance

There is always the _____ that the government will reverse its decision.

If we act now, we have a good _____ of finding a cure for the disease.

25.   priceless / worthless

_____ paintings by artists like Van Gogh should not be in the hands of private collectors.

As inflation spiralled out of control, paper money suddenly became _____ .

26.   principal(s) / principle(s)

Many people refuse to eat meat on _____ .

The _____ of the college is an ardent nonsmoker.

The country's _____ products are paper and wood.

Not many people are familiar with the _____ of nuclear physics.

27.   process / procession

The _____ made its way down the avenue.

Applying for a visa can be a long and frustrating _____ .

28.   raise / rise

As prices _____, demand usually drops.

In response to the current oil shortage, most airlines plan to _____ their fares.

29.   respectable / respectful

The delegates listened in _____ silence as the chairperson spoke.

They want to bring up their children in an area which is considered to be _____ .

30.   treat / cure

Hospitals are so understaffed in some areas that they find it almost impossible to _____ patients with minor injuries.

They were unable to _____ the disease, and hundreds died as a result.

Changes

Exercise 1. Look at these sentences and decide if the statement which follows each one is <u>true</u> or <u>false</u>. Use the words and expressions in bold to help you decide.

1. The population of the country has trebled in the last 25 years.

    *There has been a **dramatic increase** in the number of people living in the country.*

2. Unemployment has dropped by about 2% every year for the last six years.

    *There has been a **steady decrease** in the number of people out of work.*

3. The government has spent a lot of money improving roads around the state.

    *There has been a **deterioration** in the state road system.*

4. The number of exam passes achieved by the college's students has risen by almost 50%.

    *There has been a **decline** in the number of exam passes.*

5. Americans abroad have discovered that they can buy more foreign currency with their dollar.

    *There has been a **weakening** of the dollar.*

6. It is now much easier to import goods into the country than it was a few years ago.

    *There has been a **tightening up** of border controls.*

7. We're increasing our stocks of coal before the winter begins.

    *We're **running down** our stocks of coal.*

8. Prices have gone up by about 4% every year since 1998.

    *There has been a **constant rise** in the rate of inflation.*

9. The pass rate for the exam was 3% lower this year than it was last year.

    *There has been a **sharp fall** in the pass rate.*

10. The alliance are going to reduce the number of conventional weapons in their armed forces.

    *The alliance are going to **build up** the number of weapons they have.*

11. Deflation has adversely affected industries around the country.

    *There has been a **growth** in industrial activity.*

12. The rules are much stricter now than they were before.

    *There has been a **relaxation** of the rules.*

13. Last year, 12% of the population worked in industry and 10% worked in agriculture. This year, 14% of the population work in industry and 8% work in agriculture.

    *There has been a **narrowing of the gap** between those working in different sectors of the economy.*

14. Some management roles in the company will not exist this time next year.

    *Some management roles are going to be **phased out**.*

15. More people are shopping at large supermarkets rather than small corner stores.

    *There has been an **upward trend** in the number of people shopping in small corner stores.*

16. Her English is clearly better now than it was when she first arrived.

    *There has been **marked progress** in her English.*

17. People live in better houses, drive nicer cars and eat higher-quality food than they did twenty years ago.

    *There has been a **general improvement** in the standard of living.*

18. Our company has opened factories in France, Germany and Italy in the last five years.

    *Our company has witnessed considerable **expansion** in the last five years.*

19. The government will spend less on education next year.

    *There are going to be **cuts** in education spending next year.*

20. Americans nowadays want to see more of the world.

    *Americans nowadays want to **narrow** their horizons.*

Exercise 2. Check your answers, then use some of the words and expressions in bold above and in the answer key to write some sentences about your country.

Addition, equation and conclusion

This exercise will help you to review more of the important words that we use to join ideas in an essay, a verbal presentation or sometimes in everyday speech.

Exercise 1. Put the following words and expressions into their correct place in the table depending on their function.

to sum up briefly • along with • as well as • it can be concluded that • likewise • similarly • also • too • in addition • besides • to conclude • in brief • in the same way • thus • what's more • furthermore • moreover • along with • to summarize • therefore • correspondingly

Addition (For example: *and*)	Equation (For example: *equally*)	Conclusion (For example: *in conclusion*)

Exercise 2. Complete these sentences with one of the words or expressions from above. In most cases, more than one answer is possible.

1. Tourism brings much needed money to developing countries. _____, it provides employment for the local population.

2. _____ bringing much needed money to developing countries, tourism provides employment for the local population.

3. Tourists should respect the local environment. _____ they should respect the local customs.

4. _____ industrial waste, pollution from car fumes is poisoning the environment.

5. In order to travel, you need a passport. _____, you might need a visa, immunization jabs and written permission to visit certain areas.

6. Drugs are banned there - _____. weapons such as guns and knives.

7. All power corrupts. _____, absolute power corrupts absolutely.

8. You shouldn't smoke, drink, take drugs or eat unhealthy food._____., you should live a more healthy lifestyle.

9. The ozone layer is becoming depleted, the air in the cities is becoming too dirty to breathe and our seas and rivers are no longer safe to swim in. _____ pollution is slowly destroying the planet.

10. Your grades have been very poor all year. _____ you need to work really hard if you want

Working words

This exercise lets you review some of the more common uses of 'grammar'-type words (prepositions, conjunctions, pronouns, prepositions, etc) in context. Use one word to complete each gap in the sentences. In some cases, there may be more than one alternative answer, but you should just give one of them.

1. I'm afraid _____ say you have absolutely _____ chance _____ passing the exam.

2. A few years _____, people _____ to write letters to each other. _____ days, it's all e-mails and text messages.

3. You can't leave early, _____ if you promise to work late tomorrow.

4. _____ 1999 and 2003, the book sold _____ a million copies.

5. One or two of my friends live abroad, but _____ of them live _____ my home.

6. Please _____ quiet. I'm trying to concentrate _____ my project.

7. _____ it rains tomorrow, we can go _____ a picnic.

8. We wanted to see the exhibition _____ the art gallery, but _____ how many other people _____ be there, we decided to give it a miss.

9. In _____ of missing most of his lessons, he _____ to pass the exam.

10. Teachers are _____ capable of making mistakes as _____ else.

11. I adore spicy food. _____ is the reason I'm so fond _____ Mexican cooking.

12. Jan Kelly, a teacher _____ works at St Clare's in Oxford, has _____ been given a 'Teacher of the Year' award.

13. He approached his English lessons _____ enthusiasm, and _____ excellent progress as a result.

14. His sudden change of heart took everyone _____ surprise, since previously he _____ been very interested in the project.

15. He spent the second half of his life living in _____ remote town of Hogstail Common, _____ he wrote most of his novels.

16. Some people try to _____ up cigarettes by smoking _____ they feel sick, or by limiting themselves to one or _____ a day, but _____ methods are not very effective.

17. My English school, _____ is in town, is _____ of the best schools in the _____ country.

18. There were at _____ sixty people in the room, which was far _____ than the organizers expected, and _____ there were only 20 chairs, most of us _____ to stand.

19. In most respects he was a normal child, but _____ made him different _____ everybody _____ was his enthusiasm for solving complex mathematical puzzles.

Spelling

Exercise 1. There are <u>eleven</u> words in this passage which are spelled incorrectly. Can you find and correct them?

Apart from condemming tobacco companies and rising the price of cigarettes, the goverment's antismoking campain has failed to have major long-term affects, and the only people bennefitting from it are the Internal Revenue service. Meanwhile, the health service says it may refuse to treat persistant smokers. Of course, this hasn't prevented the big tobbaco companys spending vast amounts of money on advertiseing.

Exercise 2. Instructions as above

It is argueable whether good pronounciation is more important than good grammer and vocabulery. Consientious students balance their aquisition of these skills, hopeing to acheive both fluency and accuracey. Teachers should encorage there students to practice all the relevant language skills.

Exercise 3. Instructions as above.

It is becomming increasingly difficcult for many people to find decent accomodations in Los Angeles at a price they can afford. To put it simpley, most people just don't have the necesary funds. Organizeations such as Home Front can offer advise, but it widely agreed that the situation is no longer managable. The fact that the LA city council is building cheap, tempory housing for lower-paid profesionals is the only official acknowlegment of this problem.

Presenting an argument

Exercise 1. Read the text below, in which somebody is trying to decide whether to go straight to college from school, or spend a year going around the world. Put their argument into the correct order, using the key words and expressions in bold to help you. The first one and last one have been done for you.

A **(1)** I'm really in two minds about what to do when I leave school. Should I go straight to college or should I spend a year traveling around the world?

B. **It is often said that** knowledge is the key to power, and I cannot disagree with this.

C. **On the one hand**, I would experience lots of different cultures.

D. Unfortunately, **another point is that** if I spent a year traveling I would need a lot of money.

E. And I'm not alone in this opinion. **Many consider** a sound career and a good salary to be an important goal.

F. **However**, it could be argued that I would also meet lots of interesting people while I was traveling.

G. **Secondly**, if I go straight to college, I'll learn so many things that will help me in my future life.

H. **First of all**, there are so many benefits to going straight to college.

I. But **I believe that** it would be easy to make a bit while I was traveling, giving English lessons or working in hotels and stores.

J. **Moreover**, I'll be able to take part in the social activities that the college offers, and meet lots of new friends who share the same interests.

K. **The most important point is that** the sooner I get my qualifications, the quicker I'll get a job and start earning.

L. **Nevertheless**, these inconveniences would be an inevitable part of traveling and would be greatly outweighed by the other advantages.

M. **In my opinion**, starting work and making money is one of the most important things in life.

N. **On the other hand**, I could end up suffering from culture shock, homesickness and some strange tropical diseases.

O. **Furthermore**, if I spent a year traveling, I would learn more about the world.

P **(16)**   All right, I've made my mind up. Now, where's my nearest travel agency?

Exercise 2. Using the key words and expressions in bold from the last exercise, present an argument for <u>one</u> of the following issues, or choose one of the essays from the Topics section of the book:

1.   A government's main priority is to provide education for its people.
2.   The only way to save the environment is for governments to impose strict quotas on the energy we use (for example, by restricting car ownership, limiting the water we use).
3.   Satisfaction in your job is more important than the money you earn.
4.   Living in a town or city is better than living in the countryside.
5.   It is our responsibility to help or look after those less fortunate than ourselves (for example, the homeless).

Idioms and colloquialisms 1

Idioms and colloquialisms (spoken expressions) are a common feature of the TOEFL Listening Comprehension. There are a lot of them, and each one has to be learned individually. Often, but not always, it is possible to identify the meaning of an idiom or a colloquialism from the context in which it is being used.

The idioms and colloquialisms exercises in this book focus on some of the most commonly-used expressions.

Complete the expressions in bold with a word from the box. The meaning of the expression is explained in brackets after each sentence. Two words can be used more than once.

> about • ahead • all • along • as • being • best • cheer • far • fault
> fed • gear • ground • hand • head • hold • least • mind • most
> once • other • out • rid • short • tied • up • wonder • worse

---

1. Many people believe that it's _____ **time** more money was invested in education. *(it should happen now)*

2. It's better to be _____ **of time** than to leave things until the last moment. *(early)*

3. The editor knew **all** _____ that sooner or later his integrity would be questioned. *(from the beginning)*

4. For years, he was ignored. Then, **all at** _____, his theories became very popular. *(suddenly)*

5. People know that the media don't always tell the truth, but **all in** _____ they tend to believe what they read in the press. *(generally, with everything considered)*

6. The students didn't realize there was anything wrong. _____ **for** the teachers, however, they knew that there would be problems. *(concerning)*

7. There were **at** _____ 5000 signatures on the petition. *(a minimum)*

8. They had, **at the** _____, two weeks to convince everyone they were right. *(a maximum)*

9. I'm afraid you're _____ **of** luck - there are no more seats left on that flight. *(nothing left)*

10. We're rather _____ **of time** at the moment, so can't help you. *(not have enough)*

11. **By** _____ the best way to develop your English vocabulary is to read from a wide variety of sources. *(greatly)*

12. She explained she was rather _____ **up**, and asked me to come back later. *(busy)*

13. Are you still _____ **for** this weekend, or have you made other plans? *(ready to do, or interested in doing, something)*

14. When it comes to exams, most people **do their** _____ and hope they pass. *(try hard)*

15. I was going to join Professor Malkorak's class, but I've **changed my** _____. *(change an earlier decision)*

© Bloomsbury Publishing. For reference see *American English Study Dictionary* (1-901659-69-0)

16. People are becoming increasingly _____ **up with** the misuse of taxpayers' money
.   *(angry, annoyed)*

17. The best way to _____ **him up** is to take him out to dinner. *(make someone feel happy)*

18. The meetings took place **every** _____ week for almost six months. *(every second one)*

19. We finally decided to _____ **up** and do some serious work. *(start something)*

20. My English teacher suggested I **get** _____ **of** a good dictionary and grammar book.
    (obtain)

21. The plan never really **got off the** _____, and was abandoned after only two weeks. *(make a successful start)*

22. There is no point in **finding** _____ with something if you are not prepared to help improve it. *(criticize)*

23. Interstellar travel is currently not possible. **For the time** _____, we will have to make do with occasional trips into near space. *(temporarily, now)*

24. If you are not prepared to **give a** _____, you might as well leave. *(help)*

25. They **had a** _____ in ensuring that the conference was a success. *(were partly responsible)*

26. After they had **got** _____ **of** the evidence, they felt a bit more relaxed. *(discard)*

27. What I **have in** _____ for our end-of-year party is a weekend trip to Tijuana. *(plan)*

28. In the last five years, the situation has gone **from bad to** _____. *(deteriorated)*

29. **It's no** _____ he failed; he didn't do any revision. *(predictably)*

30. He **hit the nail on the** _____ when he said the teacher lacked character. *(be right about something)*

Also see: **Idioms and colloquialisms 2 - 5**

           Phrasal verbs 1 - 5

Idioms and colloquialisms 2

Complete the dialogues with an expression from the box.

Get a life! • Go for it! • How should I know? • How's it going? I couldn't agree more. • I could care less. • I don't mind I'll give it all I've got • I'm afraid it turns me off. • I'm used to it. Let me sleep on it • No way! • Never mind, it can't be helped. Not at all. • Not again! • Sure, why not? Way to go! • What a drag! • What do you have in mind? • You bet!

1. A. Shall we eat out or do you want me to cook something?
    B. _____
    A. Great. In that case, let's eat out.

2. A. The economics seminar has been cancelled.
    B. _____
    A. I'm afraid so. Professor Parkhill sure seems to be absent a lot these days.

3. A. Our history lessons are really boring, aren't they?
    B. _____
    A. Right. Perhaps we shouldn't have chosen it as an option.

4. A. We're going to Mo's bar tonight. Want to come?
    B. _____
    A. Come on, don't be like that! It'll be fun!

5. A. Are you going to join the History of Science class?
    B. _____
    A. OK, but don't wait too long. It's already filling up fast.

6. A. Aren't you interested in science?
    B. _____
    A. Me too. I find it really boring.

7. A. I spent all Sunday at home watching TV.
    B. _____
    A. I know! I really should get out more.

8. A. If you don't work harder, you'll fail your exams.
    B. _____
    A. Well, you should. Your whole future might depend on them.

9. A. I've passed all my exams - grade A's all round!
    B. _____
    A. Thanks. I never thought I'd be able to do it.

10. A. Do you think I should apply to the University of West Virginia?
    B. _____
    A. All right, I will. Thanks.

11. A. Thank you so much for all your help. I couldn't have done it without you.
     B. _____
     A. No, really, I really appreciate it.

12. A. I'm really sorry that I lost your dictionary.
     B. _____
     A. Nevertheless, I promise to replace it.

13. A. Can I have a look at your essay to get a few ideas?
     B. _____
     A. Thanks. I'll do the same for you next time.

14. A. I'm working real hard for my exam at the moment.
     B. _____
     A. Oh, not bad. I'm fairly confident of passing.

15. A. Where's Murai today?
     B. _____
     A. Don't be like that. I was only asking.

16. A. We need to finish this assignment by Monday. There goes our weekend.
     B. _____
     A. I know, but we'll make up for it next weekend.

17. A. Want to come to the concert tonight?
     B . _____
     A. That's great. I'll go and get us some tickets.

18. A. Do you think you'll pass your exams?
     B. _____
     A. That's the spirit! Well, good luck.

19. A. Do you find it difficult getting up at 6 o'clock every morning?
     B. _____
     A. I suppose you must be. You've been doing it for so long.

20. A. We're thinking of doing something to celebrate the end of the semester.
     B. _____
     A. I'm not sure, really. Perhaps a barbecue, or something like that.

Also see: **Idioms and colloquialisms 1, 3 - 5**
             Phrasal verbs 1 - 5

51

Idioms and colloquialisms 3

Exercise A.
The colloquial expressions in bold have been used in the wrong dialogues. Rearrange them so that they are in the correct dialogues.

1. Would you mind looking after my bag while I go to the rest room?
    A little bird told me.

2. Do you mind if I sit here?
    I'm keeping my fingers crossed.

3. How do you know the test has been cancelled?
    Be my guest!

4. I'd be really grateful if you didn't tell anyone about it.
    Fire away. I'm all ears.

5. Do you think you'll pass the exam?
    Rather you than me.

6. I've signed up for extra Sociology classes with Professor Dullman.
    Now you're talking!

7. I've got some really interesting news.
    I'm having second thoughts.

8. You don't want to work tonight? OK, let's go to the theater instead.
    That'll be the day!

9. I thought you were going to apply for a place on the Theory of Knowledge course.
    I'd be glad to.

10. I promise to work harder from now on.
    My lips are sealed.

Exercise B.
Instructions as above.

1. I can't afford to go to the concert tonight.
    I'd love to.

2. I've managed to get a place on the Advanced Studies program.
    You're welcome.

3. Would you like to come to Gino's tonight?
    Yes. Take care and keep in touch.

4. Thank you very much for all your help.
    Congratulations.

© Bloomsbury Publishing. For reference see *American English Study Dictionary* (1-901659-69-0)

5.   Oh wow! What a great room. It's wonderful.
       Couldn't be better.

6.   Come on! Hurry up!
       I'd rather you didn't.

7.   It's been nice seeing you again. Let's get together again soon.
       Hold on.

8.   Hi, Tom. How are you?
       Oh, that's too bad.

9.   Do you mind if I smoke in here?
       Oh, this is on me.

10.   I didn't do too well in the end of semester exams.
       Thanks. Make yourself at home.

Exercise C.
Instructions as above.

1.   I'm about halfway through my essay.
       I'll say

2.   I thought the lecture on the Declaration of Independence was great. Did you enjoy it?
       That's a load off my mind.

3.   Snake is considered a delicacy in some countries. Would you ever consider eating it?
       Of course. Take a seat.

4.   Professor de Gruchy has extended the deadline for our essays to Thursday, so you don't need
       to worry about not finishing it on time.
       Cheer up. It's not the end of the world.

5.   Did you know that our economics teacher has left the questions for tomorrow's test lying on
       his desk?
       Well, take it easy. Don't kill yourself.

6.   Could you give me a bit of help with this assignment?
       Have a good time.

7.   Can I come in?
       How's it going?

8.   I've got so much to do by Monday; two essays to write, a presentation to prepare, and I have
       to do some research on the history of the UN.
       Well, keep it to yourself.

9.   I'm so depressed. That's the third time I've failed my driving test.
       Sure thing.

10.   I'm off to Niagara Falls for the weekend. See you Monday.
       No way!

Also see: **Idioms and colloquialisms 1, 2, 4, 5**
              Phrasal verbs 1 - 5

Idioms and colloquialisms 4

Connect the first part of the sentence on this page with the second half on the next page. Use the expressions in bold to help you make the connection.

1.   If you come late, could you please **let me**...

2.   I was rather unhappy when she **made a**...

3.   The project was **more or**...

4.   I just need to complete this assignment, and then my coursework will be over **once and**...

5.   His lectures are generally really dull, but **once in**...

6.   I've never been **too**...

7.   There are parts of the course which are a little boring, but **on the**...

8.   Don't try to do everything at once. Try to do things **step by**...

9.   There's a chance that **sooner or**...

10.   When you first start a new job, it can take a while to **learn the**...

11.   I know you have a lot of work, but **look on the bright** ...

12.   The CEO can't be **in his right**...

13.   You shouldn't **go over his**...

14.   You're joking. You're **pulling my**...

15.   It can be difficult to **make ends**...

16.   Try to **make the most of your**...

17.   I asked Ron to get the computer fixed, and he promised to **take**...

18.   I understand the theory, but I **get mixed**...

19.   Don't worry about the exam. Just **give it**...

20.   I'm not sure whether to take a vacation this summer. I'll decide **one way or**...

21.   I wasn't sure whether to apply for a PhD course, but in the end I decided to **go**...

22.   I got a grade A for my first assignment of the year. That's **a good**...

Idioms and colloquialisms 4

A. ...**big** on science; I've always preferred the arts.

B. ...**whole** it's really good.

C. ...**start**, isn't it?

D. ...**all you've got** and hope for the best.

E. ...**for all**. It'll be a real relief.

F. ...**mind**, making a stupid decision like that.

G. ...**step** until you've finished.

H. ...**up** when I try to describe it on paper.

I. ...**the other** when I see my exam results.

J. ...**care of it** at the earliest opportunity.

K. ...**leg**. Right?

L. ...**for it** and see what happens.

M. ...**meet** when you're a student on a low income.

N. ...**later** the students will demand some real changes.

O. ...**ropes** and become familiar with the way things work.

P. ...**head** and make your own decisions.

Q. ...**point of** reminding me about my previous bad grades.

R. ...**less** complete when someone pointed out they had missed some details.

S. ...**know** in advance.

T. ...**time** when you're in New York.

U. ...**side**; at least you won't get bored this weekend!

V. ...**a while** there's something of interest.

Also see: **Idioms and colloquialisms 1, 2 , 3.**

Phrasal verbs 1 - 5

Idioms and colloquialisms 5

Choose the correct underlined word to complete each of the idioms in bold. The meaning of each idiom is in brackets after the sentence.

1. You shouldn't try to **burn the match / lighter / candle at both ends**; you'll exhaust yourself. *(to get up early in the morning and go to bed late at night on a regular basis)*

2. Once he started looking into the details, he realized what a **can of worms / beans / beer** they were opening. *(a difficult and complicated situation)*

3. It was a difficult decision, but he decided to take the **goat / cow / bull by the horns** and tell his boss that he wanted to leave the company. *(to deal bravely or confidently with a difficult situation)*

4. Some insurance companies make their customers **pay through the ears / nose / mouth** for their services. *(pay a lot of money)*

5. He knew that what they were doing was wrong, but **turned a blind / closed / cold eye** to it. *(to pretend not to notice, to ignore)*

6. Many people like to get **off the beaten road / path / track** when they take a vacation. *(somewhere quiet, where not a lot of people go)*

7. If you're **pressed / crushed / squeezed for time**, we can talk later. *(busy, in a hurry)*

8. I've been feeling a bit **under the thumb / weather / table** recently, but I'm feeling better now. *(slightly ill)*

9. He's a rather boring person, but **once in a blue / red / green moon**, he'll come out with something really amazing. *(very rarely)*

10. He gave us some information that was strictly **off the books / record / list**. *(unofficial, to be kept secret)*

11. We don't want to **lose land / ground / place** in the baseball competition. *(become less successful than the others)*

12. Let's have a party at the beginning of the year. It will help to **break the ice / mold / air**. *(make people feel more friendly and willing to talk to each other)*

Idioms and colloquialisms 5

13. Everybody should say exactly how they feel. That should **clear the** <u>room / air / feelings</u>. *(to help end an argument or disagreement)*

14. It's very rude to **talk** <u>store / work / jobs</u> when you're out with other people. *(to discuss your job with a colleague, usually in a social situation where there are others present)*

15. Don't let him stop you; **stand your** <u>land / place / ground</u> and tell him you won't change your mind. *(refuse to change your mind about something, even when people oppose you)*

16. I only just passed my exam. It was a very <u>far / close / exact</u> **thing**. *(something almost did or didn't happen)*

17. What's happened? **Put me in the** <u>picture / story / scene</u>. *(let somebody know what has happened, usually when other people already know)*

18. You've really **made a** <u>name / title / place</u> for yourself, haven't you? *(to become well known, famous and / or respected)*

19. Have you seen his house? It's **out of this** <u>planet / earth / world</u>. *(extremely good, wonderful, etc)*

20. He knew I was friendly with his boss, and asked me to **pull a few** <u>legs / strings / ropes</u> for him.   *(to use your influence with somebody in order to get something)*

21. Donna **<u>played / did / went</u> hooky** again today; that's the third lecture she's missed this week. *(to miss a lesson, class, etc, for no good reason)*

22. My bank account's **in the** <u>black / red / pink</u> again. *(to owe money to the bank because you're spent too much)*

23. I've completed three out of my five assignments already. **So far, so** <u>good / fine / acceptable</u>. *(until now, everything is going well)*

24. I'm really angry with Jerry. It's time I **had it** <u>in / out / over</u> with him. *(to tell somebody you are angry with them, and explain why).*

25. His theories **broke fresh** <u>earth / ground / land</u> and changed the way people thought about science. *(do something original or innovative)*

Topics

This section is topic-specific, and focuses on some of the topics that regularly appear in the TOEFL® test. Each topic is accompanied by a typical TOEFL® Writing question, which will give you the chance to use the key vocabulary in an essay.

Children and the family

Exercise 1. Vocabulary Bank. Use your dictionary to check the meanings of any words or expressions that you don't know.

adolescence • adolescent • authoritarian • birth rate • bring up • dependant
dependent • divorced • extended (family) • family life • formative years
foster (verb) • foster child • foster family • freedom • juvenile • juvenile
delinquency • lenient • minor (noun) • nuclear (family) • nurture
overprotective • protective • raise • rebellious • relationship • relatives
responsible • siblings • single parent • single-parent family
strict • supervision • run wild • upbringing • well-adjusted

Exercise 2. Complete this case study with appropriate words and expressions from the Vocabulary Bank. You may need to change the form of some of the words.

Bob's problems began during his 1............... years. His parents got 2............... when he was young, and neither of his parents wanted to raise him or his brother and sister, so he was 3............... by a 4............... chosen by his parent's social worker. Unfortunately, his foster father was a strict 5............... and often beat him. Bob rebelled against this strict 6..............., and by the time he was eight, he was already 7..............., stealing from shops and playing hooky. By the time he reached 8..............., sometime around his thirteenth birthday, he had already appeared in court several times, charged with 9............... The judge blamed his foster parents, explaining that children needed 10............... parents and guardians who would look after them properly. The foster father objected to this, pointing out that Bob's 11............... - his two brothers and sister - were 12............... children who behaved at home and worked well at school.

This has raised some interesting questions about the modern family system. While it is true that parents should not be too 13............... with children by letting them do what they want when they want, or be too 14............... by sheltering them from the realities of life, it is also true that they should not be too strict. It has also highlighted the disadvantages of the modern 15............... family where the child has only its mother and father to rely on (or the 16............... family, in which the mother or father has to struggle particularly hard to support their 17...............). In fact, many believe that we should return to traditional family values and the 18............... family: extensive research has shown that children from these families are generally better behaved and have a better chance of success in later life.

Exercise 3. Now try this essay. Use words and expressions from the Vocabulary Bank, and any other words or expressions that you think would be relevant.

Some people believe that children nowadays have too much freedom. Others believe that children are protected too much by their parents. Which of these statements do you agree with? Use specific reasons and examples to support your decision.

60

Exercise 1. Vocabulary Bank. Use your dictionary to check the meanings of any words or expressions that you don't know.

acquire • distance learning course • course • degree • discipline • doctorate
elementary (education) • elementary school • enrol • exam • experience
faculty • fail • grades • grade school • graduate (noun) • graduate (verb)
graduate school • grant • higher degree • higher education • high school
junior high school • kindergarten • learn • learning resources center • lecture
lecturer • lesson • literacy • middle school • class • numeracy
online • opportunity • pass • physical education • private school • professor
• public school • qualifications • resit (an exam) • resources
secondary (education) • semester • seminar • SAT® (Scholastic Aptitude Test)
sit / take (an exam) • skills • study • subject
syllabus • topic • tutor • tutorial • undergraduate • vocational

Exercise 2. Complete this essay with appropriate words and expressions from the Vocabulary Bank. You may need to change the form of some of the words.

'You are never too old to learn'. Do you agree with this statement?

Education is a long process that not only provides us with basic (1).......... such as (2).......... and (3).........., but is also essential in shaping our future lives. From the moment we enter (4).......... as 5-year-olds, and as we progress through (5).......... and (6).......... education, we are laying the foundations for the life ahead of us. We must (7).......... ourselves to work hard so that we can (8).......... exams and gain the (9).......... we will need to secure a good job. We must also (10).......... valuable life skills so that we can fit in and work with those around us. And of course (11).......... helps us to develop our bodies and stay fit and healthy.

For most people, this process ends when they are in their mid-to-late teens and they (12).......... from high school. For others, however, it is the beginning of a lifetime of learning. After they finish school, many progress to (13).......... education where they will work toward a (14).......... in a chosen (15).......... at college. After that, they may work for a while before opting to study at a (16).......... for a Masters degree, or a (17)............ Alternatively, they may choose to attend an (18).......... after work. And if they live a long way from a college or university, they might follow a (19).......... using mail and the Internet. In fact, it is largely due to the proliferation of computers that many people who have not been near a school for many years have started to study again and can gain qualifications (20)............. .

We live in a fascinating and constantly changing world, and we must continually learn and acquire new knowledge if we are to adapt and keep up with changing events. Our schooldays are just the beginning of this process, and we should make the best of every (21).......... to develop ourselves, whether we are eighteen or eighty. You are, indeed, never too old to learn.

Exercise 3. Now try this essay. Use words and expressions from the Vocabulary Bank, and any other words or expressions that you think would be relevant.

Do you agree with this statement? 'The most important things in life are not learned at school or college'.

Use examples and details in your answer.

Food and diet

Exercise 1. Vocabulary Bank. Use your dictionary to check the meanings of any words or expressions that you don't know.

allergy • allergic • anorexia • balanced diet • bulimia • calories
carbohydrates • cholesterol • consume • consumption • diet (noun + verb)
eating disorder • fast food • fat • fiber • food poisoning • free range
genetically modified • harvest • health food • listeria
malnutrition • malnourished • minerals • nutrition • nutritious • obese
obesity • organic • overweight • protein • salmonella • scarce
scarcity • underweight • vegan • vegetarian • vitamins

Exercise 2. Complete this essay with appropriate words and expressions from the Vocabulary Bank. You may need to change the form of some of the words.

'Despite the huge variety of foods in our supermarkets, it is becoming increasingly difficult to eat a healthy diet'. Do you agree? Support your opinion by using specific reasons and examples.

Most children enjoy eating 1................, but scientific tests have shown us that burgers and pizzas can lack essential 2................ and 3................ which are essential for health and growth, while simultaneously containing large amounts of 4................ and 5................ which can result in obesity and heart problems. Many children end up suffering from 6................, since they eat too much of the wrong sort of food. In fact, in many areas of the developed world, a lot of children show similar symptoms to those in poorer developing countries, where 7................ of food causes thousands of deaths from starvation, especially in the wake of natural disasters which ruin crops and in some cases totally destroy the annual 8................

Dietitians tell us that we must eat a 9................, as it is essential we consume sufficient quantities of the different food groups. They tell us that we should all eat more 10................, which cannot be digested by the body, and fewer foods which are high in 11................, as this can block the walls of arteries and lead to heart problems. This is good advice, of course, but our lifestyles often make this difficult. Many of the ready-prepared foods we buy from supermarkets are high in 12................, giving us more energy than we actually need. 13................ foods are appearing on our supermarket shelves, even though nobody is really sure if altering the composition of food cells is safe. We have the option, of course, of buying 14................ foods, but naturally-cultivated fruits and vegetables are expensive. And to make matters worse, we are continually hearing about outbreaks of 15................ and 16................ which put us off eating certain foods, as nobody wants to spend time in the hospital suffering from 17................

A few things to watch out for next time you go shopping. If you have the time and the money, that is!

Exercise 3. Now try this essay. Use words and expressions from the Vocabulary Bank, and any other words or expressions that you think would be relevant.

'If food tastes good, it's probably bad for you'. How far do you agree with this statement? Use specific reasons and examples to support your opinion.

The media

Exercise 1. Vocabulary Bank. Use your dictionary to check the meanings of any words or expressions that you don't know.

audience • broadcast • cable • censorship • channel
checkbook • circulation • editor • journalism • coverage • current affairs
download • entertainment • exploit • feature • freedom of the press • the
gutter press • honest • information • information overload
invasion of privacy • journalists • libel • log on • media tycoon
paparazzi • the press • program • read between the lines • readership
reporters • tabloids • the Internet • unscrupulous • web • website

Exercise 2. Read this essay and complete the gaps with one of the words or expressions from the Vocabulary Bank. You may need to change the form of some of the words.

'The media plays a valuable role in keeping us informed and entertained. However, many people believe it has too much power and freedom'. Do you agree?'

Barely a hundred years ago, if we wanted to stay informed about what was going on in the world, we had to rely on word of mouth or, at best, newspapers. But because communication technology was very basic, the news we received was often days or weeks old.

We still have newspapers, of course, but they have changed almost beyond recognition. Whether we choose to read the top newspapers with their quality 1........ of news and other 1........ by top 3.......... and articles by acclaimed 4.........., or if we prefer the popular 5.........., with their lively gossip and colorful stories, we are exposed to a wealth of information barely conceivable at the beginning of the last century.

We also have television and radio. News 6........ let us know about world events practically as they happen, while sitcoms, talk shows and documentaries, etc. especially on 7............. television keep us entertained and informed. And there is also the 8........, where we can access information from millions of 9.......... around the world which we can then 10.......... onto our own computers.

However, these forms of 11.......... and 12.......... (or 'infotainment' as they are now sometimes collectively called) have their negative side. Famous personalities frequently accuse the 13.......... (and sometimes even respectable papers) of 14.......... by the 15.......... who are determined to get a story at any cost. Newspapers are often accused of 16.......... by angry politicians who dislike reading lies about themselves, and there are frequent accusations of 17.........., with 18.......... reporters paying people to create stories for their newspapers or television programes. Of course, it is not just the papers which are to blame. Sex and violence are increasing on the television. Undesirable people fill the 19.......... with equally undesirable material which can be accessed by anyone with a home computer. And the fear of 20.......... prevents many from 21.......... to the Internet.

Many argue that the government should impose stricter 22.......... to prevent such things happening. But others argue that 23.......... is the keystone of a free country. Personally, I take the view that while the media may occasionally abuse its position of power, the benefits greatly outweigh the disadvantages. Our lives would be much emptier without the wealth of information available to us today, and we are better people as a result.

Exercise 3. Now try this essay. Use words and expressions from the Vocabulary Bank, and any other words or expressions that you think would be relevant.

'What are the qualities or features of a good newspaper, current affairs television program or news website?' Use specific details and examples to explain your answer.

63

Money and finance

Exercise 1. Vocabulary Bank. Use your dictionary to check the meanings of any words or expressions that you don't know.

a bank • a bargain • to be broke • to be bankrupt • cash
check • the cost of living • credit card • to credit • a debt
to debit • to deposit money • a discount • distribution of wealth
dividends • economical • to economize • exorbitant • expenditure
extravagant • frugal • income • income tax • inflation • inherit
interest • to invest • an investment • a loan • make a loss
make a profit • the market • a mortgage • on credit • an overdraft
overpriced • a pension • priceless • a reduction • a refund
salary • to save • savings • shares • stocks
tax / rent (etc) rebate • unemployment / housing / child (etc) welfare • wage •
wealthy • welfare • to withdraw money • worthless

Exercise 2. Complete this dialogue with appropriate words and expressions from the Vocabulary Bank. You may need to change the form of some of the words.

<u>'Financial advice from a father to a son'</u>

In the play 'Hamlet' by William Shakespeare, a father gives his son some financial advice. *'Neither a borrower nor a lender be'*, he says. He is trying to tell his son that he should never 1.............. money from anyone because it will make it difficult for him to manage his finances. Likewise he should never give a financial 2.............. to a friend because he will probably never see the money again, and will probably lose his friend as well.

The play was written over four hundred years ago, but today many parents would give similar advice to their children. Imagine the conversation they would have now:

Jim: Right dad, I'm off to college now.

Dad: OK son, but let me give you some sound financial advice before you go.

Jim: Oh come on dad.....

Dad: Now listen, this is important. The first thing you should do is to make sure you balance your 3.............. - the money you receive from me and mom - and your 4.............. - the money you spend. If you spend too much, you will end up with an 5.............. at the bank. Don't expect me to pay it for you.

Jim: But it's so difficult. Things are so expensive, and the 6.............. goes up all the time. 7.............. is running at about 10%.

Dad: I know, but you should try to 8.............. . Avoid expensive stores and restaurants. Also, leave your money in a good 9.............. account . Also, avoid buying things 10..............

Jim: Why?

Dad: Because stores charge you an 11.............. amount of money to buy things over a period of time. It's much better to 12.............. a little bit of money each week so that when you see something you want, you can buy it outright. Try to wait for the sales, when stores offer huge 13.............. and you can pick up a 14.............. And try to get a 15..............

Jim: How do I do that?

Dad: Easy. When you buy something, ask the store if they'll lower the price by, say, 10%. Next, when you eventually get a job and are earning a good salary, try to 16.............. the money in a good company. Buy 17.............. in government organizations or 18.............. in private companies.

Jim: OK dad, I've heard enough. Thanks for the advice.

Exercise 3. Now try this essay. Use words and expressions from the Vocabulary Bank, and any other words or expressions that you think would be relevant.

Some people say that 'Money makes the world go round'; others say that 'Money is the root of all evil'. Which of these do you agree with? Use examples and details in your answer.

Nature and the environment

topics

Exercise 1. Vocabulary Bank. Use your dictionary to check the meanings of any words or expressions that you don't know.

acid rain • activists • animal rights • biodegradable (packaging) • breeding (in) captivity • CFC gases • conservation • conserve • conservation programe • contaminated • degradation • desertification • ecological • ecology ecosystem • emissions • endangered species • environmentalists • erosion extinct • fossil fuels • fumes • genetically modified • global warming factory farming • greenhouse effect • greenhouse gases • natural behavior natural resources • ocean • organic • organic farming • ozone layer poaching • pollute • pollution • rare breeds • rainforest • to recycle • research solar power • tidal energy • toxic waste • unleaded fuel • wildlife management

Exercise 2. Read this essay and complete the gaps with one of the words or expressions from the Vocabulary Bank. You may need to change the form of some of the words.

'Environmental degradation is a major world problem. What causes this problem, and what can we do to prevent it?'

There is no doubt that the environment is in trouble. Factories burn 1............... that produce 2..............., and this kills trees. At the same time, 3............... rise into the air and contribute to 4..............., which threatens to melt the polar ice cap. Meanwhile farmers clear huge areas of 5............... in places such as the Amazon to produce feeding land for cattle or produce wood for building. Rivers and oceans are so heavily 6............... by industrial waste that it is no longer safe to go swimming. Cars pump out poisonous 7............... which we all have to breathe in. 8............... and overfishing are killing off millions of animals, including whales, elephants and other 9............... In fact, all around us, all living things large and small that comprise our finely balanced 10............... are being systematically destroyed by human greed and thoughtlessness.

There is a lot we can all do, however, to help prevent this. The easiest thing, of course, is to 11............... waste material such as paper and glass so that we can use it again. We should also check that the things we buy from supermarkets are packaged in 12............... packaging which decomposes easily. At the same time, we should make a conscious effort to avoid foods which are 13............... (at least until someone proves that they are safe both for us and for the environment). If you are truly committed to protecting the environment, of course, you should only buy 14............... fruit and vegetables, safe in the knowledge that they have been naturally cultivated. Finally, of course, we should buy a smaller car that uses 15............... which is less harmful to the environment or, even better, make more use of public transportation.

The serious 16..............., however, do much more. They are aware of the global issues involved and will actively involve themselves in 17............... by making sure our forests are kept safe for future generations. They will oppose activities that are harmful to animals, such as 18............... And they will campaign to keep the 19............... around our coastline free from pollution.

We cannot all be as committed as them, but we can at least make our own contribution at grassroots level. We, as humans, have inherited the earth, but that doesn't mean we can do whatever we like with it.

Exercise 3. Now try this essay. Use words and expressions from the Vocabulary Bank, and any other words or expressions that you think would be relevant.

Some people think that the government should spend as much money as possible on protecting the environment. Others think this money should be spent on other things such as education and healthcare. Which one of these opinions do you agree with? Use specific reasons and details to support your answer.

65

© Bloomsbury Publishing. For reference see *English Study Dictionary* (1-901659-61-3)

On the road

Exercise 1. Vocabulary Bank. Use your dictionary to check the meanings of any words or expressions that you don't know.

accelerate • accident • accident risk • auto theft • back out
bicycle lane • brake • congestion • crosswalk • cut in (in a vehicle)
destination • dominate • drunk driving • driver • driver's license • driving test
fatalities • a fine • freeway • highway • highway patrol • injuries
intersection • interstate • joyriding • mobility • overtake
park and ride • pedestrian • pedestrian mall • pollution
public transportation • pull in • pull over • road rage • roadwork
safety island • sidewalk • to speed • speed limit • subsidized (eg, bus services)
to tailgate • traffic light / signal • traffic calming • traffic circle / rotary
traffic-free zone • traffic jam • traffic school • transportation strategy • turnpike

Exercise 2. Complete this article with appropriate words and expressions from the Vocabulary Bank. You may need to change the form of some of the words.

1............... and 2............... on our roads are increasing from year to year: last year, 2,827 people were killed and almost 300,000 hurt in traffic-related accidents. Most of these were caused by drivers 3............... in built-up areas, where many seem to disregard the 30mph 4..............., or 5..............., especially around the Fourth of July and Thanksgiving, when more alcohol is consumed than at any other time. In many cases, it is 6............... who are the victims, knocked down as they are walking across the street at 7............... by drivers who seem to have forgotten that a red 8............... means 'Stop.'

But these innocent victims, together with the help of the highway patrol and local safety groups, are fighting back. In New Stockholm, a city plagued by 9............... and 10............... caused by traffic, and notorious for 11............... involving pedestrians and cyclists, the city council has recently implemented its new 12..............., which has improved the flow of traffic to the benefit of those on foot or on two wheels. 13............... measures such as speed bumps have slowed traffic down. 14............... programes have helped reduce the number of cars in the city, as office workers and shoppers leave their cars outside the city and bus in instead. Harley Street, the main shopping thoroughfare, has been designated a 15..............., closed to all vehicles during the day. There are more 16............... on main routes into the city, making it safer for the huge number of students and residents who rely on bicycles to get around. And 17............... public transportation has helped to keep down the cost of using buses. Meanwhile, the police and the courts are coming down hard on drivers who misuse the roads, handing down large 18............... or even jail sentences on selfish, inconsiderate drivers who believe it is their right to 19............... the roads; for these people, 20. .... is not offered as a softer alternative.

Exercise 3. Now try this essay. Use words and expressions from the Vocabulary Bank, and any other words or expressions that you think would be relevant.

Do you agree or disagree with the following statement? 'It is time we all relied less on private motor vehicles to get around, and instead used other forms of transportation'. Use specific examples and details to support your answer.

Science and technology

Exercise 1. Vocabulary Bank. Use your dictionary to check the meanings of any words or expressions that you don't know.

analyze • bioclimatology • biology • breakthrough • chemistry • computers control • cryogenics • cybernetics • development • discover • discovery e-mail • experiment • genetic engineering • genetic modification information technology • innovation • the Internet • invent • invention life expectancy • microchip • modified • molecular biology • nuclear engineering • physics • research • safeguards • technophile • technophobe

Exercise 2. Complete this essay with appropriate words and expressions from the Vocabulary Bank. You may need to change the form of some of the words.

'Science and technology have come a long way in the last 60 years, and our lives have become better as a result'. Do you agree with this statement?

The second half of the twentieth century saw more changes than in the previous two hundred years. Penicillin has already been 1............... and used to treat infections; there have been many remarkable advances in medicine that have helped to increase our average 2............... way beyond that of our ancestors. Incredible 3............... such as television have changed the way we spend our leisure hours. Perhaps the most important 4..............., however, has been the microchip. Nobody could have imagined, when it was first 5..............., that within a matter of years, this tiny piece of silicon and circuitry would be found in almost every household object from the toaster to the video recorder. And nobody could have predicted the sudden proliferation of computers that would completely change our lives, allowing us to access information from the other side of the world via the 6............... or send messages around the world by 7............... at the touch of a button. Meanwhile, 8............... into other aspects of information technology is making it easier and cheaper for us to talk to friends and relatives around the world. Good news for 9............... who love modern technology, bad news for the 10............... who would prefer to hide from these modern miracles.

But everything has a price. The development of 11............... led to mass automation in factories, which in turn led to millions losing their jobs. The genius of Einstein led to the horrors of the atomic bomb and the dangerous uncertainties of 12............... (we hear of accidents and mishaps at nuclear power stations around the world, where 13............... to prevent accidents were inadequate). The relatively new science of 14............... has been seen as a major step forward, but putting modified foods onto the market before scientists had properly 15............... them was perhaps one of the most irresponsible decisions of the 1990s. Meanwhile, pharmaceutical companies continue to 16............... on animals, a move that many consider to be cruel and unnecessary.

Of course we all rely on modern science and technology to improve our lives. However, we need to make sure that we 17. .... it rather than the other way around.

Exercise 3. Now try this essay. Use words and expressions from the Vocabulary Bank, and any other words or expressions that you think would be relevant.

What, in your opinion, has been the single most important scientific or technological development of the last fifty years? Use specific reasons and details to support your answer.

City life and country life

Exercise 1. Vocabulary Bank. Use your dictionary to check the meanings of any words or expressions that you don't know.

agriculture • amenities • apartment block • arable land • atmosphere to breed crime • Central Business District (CBD) • commute • commuter • commuter belt • congestion • construction • cosmopolitan • cost of living • crops crowded • cultivation • cultural events • construction site • depopulation development • drug abuse • employment • environment • facilities fields • green belt • industry • infrastructure • housing project • inner city lively • mall / shopping mall • melting pot • metropolis • migration • nature nightlife • outskirts • peaceful • peak period • pedestrian precinct pollution • population • population explosion • poverty • productive land property prices • prospects • resident • residential area • rural rush hour • slum • street crime • stressful • suburbs traffic jam • unemployment • urban • urban lifestyle • urban sprawl

Exercise 2. Complete this essay with appropriate words and expressions from the Vocabulary Bank. You may need to change the form of some of the words.

Describe a place where you live or have lived, outlining its good points and bad points.

For seven years I lived in Singapore, a 1............... of almost three million people. Like London, Paris and New York, Singapore is a 2............... city, with people from different parts of the world living and working together. I enjoyed the 3............... lifestyle I led there, and made the most of the superb 4..............., ranging from the excellent stores to some of the best restaurants in the world. In the evenings and at weekends there were always 5...............; with such diverse attractions as classical western music, an exhibition of Malay art or a Chinese opera in the street, it was difficult to get bored. Perhaps most impressive, however, was the remarkable transportation 6..............., with excellent roads, a swift and efficient bus service and a state-of-the-art subway system that could whisk 7............... from the suburbs straight into the heart of the city (this was particularly important, as the government banned private cars from entering the 8............... during the morning and afternoon 9............... in order to reduce 10............... on the roads and 11............... from the exhausts.

Of course, living in a city like this has its disadvantages as well. For a start, the 12............... can be very high - renting an apartment, for example, is very expensive. And as the city is expanding, there are a lot of 13............... where new apartments are continually being built to deal with the 14................ that is a direct result of the government encouraging people to have more children.

Fortunately, Singapore doesn't suffer from problems that are common in many cities such as 15..............., which is partly the result of the government imposing very severe penalties on anyone bringing narcotics into the country, so it is safe to walk the streets at night. In fact, the 16............... housing projects there are probably the safest and most orderly in the world.

Singapore wouldn't be ideal for everyone, however, especially if you come from the countryside and are used to a 17............... lifestyle. The traditional villages that were once common have disappeared as the residents there realized there were no 18............... for their future and moved into new government housing in the city. Nowadays, there is very little 19............... around the city, which means that Singapore imports almost all of its food. And despite a 'green' approach to city planning, the 20............... that has eaten into the countryside has had a detrimental effect on the 21.................

Exercise 3. Now try this essay. Use words and expressions from the Vocabulary Bank, and any other words or expressions that you think would be relevant.

Some people prefer to live in the countryside or in a small town. Others prefer to live in a big city. Which place would you prefer to live in? Use specific reasons and details to support your answer.

Exercise 1. Vocabulary Bank. Use your dictionary to check the meanings of any words or expressions that you don't know.

to acclimatize • an alien • all-inclusive • business class • check-in to check into (a hotel) • to check out (of a hotel) • coach class • a cruise culture shock • to deport / be deported • to disembark • economic migrants ecotourism • to embark • an embassy • to emigrate / emigration • an excursion an expatriate • first class • an illegal alien • immigration • an independent traveler • internally displaced • a journey • a long-haul flight • mass tourism a migrant • a package tour • a package tourist • a passport • persona non grata a refugee • to repatriate • a safari • a short-haul flight • a tour operator • a travel agency • a trip • the UNHCR • a visa • a voyage

Exercise 2. Read this essay and complete the gaps with one of the words or expressions from the Vocabulary Bank. You may need to change the form of some of the words.

'There are two types of traveler: those who do it because they want to, and those who do it because they have to'. Discuss this statement, using specific examples.

Most of us have, at some point in our lives, experienced the joys of travel. We go to the 1............... to pick up our brochures. We book a two-week 2............... with flights and accommodations included, (or if we are 3..............., we make our own way to the country and travel around from place to place with a backpack). We make sure we have all the right currency, our passport and any 4............... that are necessary to get us into the country. We go to the airport and 5............... We strap ourselves into our tiny 6............. aircraft seats and a few hours later we 7............... from the aircraft, strange new sights, smells and sounds greeting us. Nowadays, it seems, the whole world goes on vacation at once: the age of 8............... is in full swing!

But for the great majority of people around the world, travel for them is done in the face of great adversity and hardship. They never get to indulge in an 9............... vacation in a luxury hotel with all meals and drinks included. They never get to explore the lush Amazon rain forest or the frozen wastes of the Arctic on an 10............... vacation. For them, travel is a matter of life and death. I refer, of course, to all the 11............... escaping from their own countries, or the 12..............., moved from one part of their country to another by an uncaring government, or 13............... forced to find a job and seek a living wherever they can.

Can you imagine anything worse than the misery these people must face? Let's not confuse them with those 14............... , who choose to live in another country and often have nice houses and high salaries. These people are simply desperate to survive. As well as losing their homes because of war or famine or other natural disasters, they must come to terms with their new environment: for many, the 15............... can be too great. And while many countries with an open policy on 16............... will welcome them in with open arms, others will simply turn them away. These people become 17..............., unwanted and unwelcome. Even if they manage to get into a country, they will often be 18............... or repatriated. Their future is uncertain.

Something to think about, perhaps, the next time you are 19............... to your five-star hotel by a palm-fringed beach or sitting in a bus on an 20............... to a tourist attraction.

Exercise 3. Now try this essay. Use words and expressions from the Vocabulary Bank, and any other words or expressions that you think would be relevant.

What are the good things and bad things about traveling? Use specific examples to explain your answer.

Work

adverse working conditions • applicant • be laid off • benefits • blue-collar worker • candidate • commission • demanding • dismiss dismissal • downsizing • employee • employer • fire • fixed income freelance • full time • hire • incentives • incentive plan • income interview • interviewee • interviewer • job satisfaction job security • manager • manual worker • manufacturing industry • (on) leave overtime • part-time • payraise • pension • pension contributions • perks pressure • profession • promotion • recruitment drive • resign • salary self-employed • semiskilled • service industry • sick building syndrome • sick pay skilled • a steady job • stress • supervisor • unemployed • union • unskilled • unsociable hours • wages • (on) welfare • white-collar worker • workaholic

Exercise 2. Complete this essay with appropriate words and expressions from the Vocabulary Bank. You may need to change the form of some of the words.

Some people live to work and others work to live. In most cases, this depends on the job they have and the conditions under which they are employed. In your opinion, what are the elements that make a job worthwhile?

In answering this question, I would like to look first at the elements that combine to make a job undesirable. By avoiding such factors, potential 1.......... are more likely to find a job that is more worthwhile, and by doing so, hope to achieve happiness in their work.

First of all, it doesn't matter if you are an 2.......... worker cleaning the floor, a 3.......... 4.......... worker on a production line in one of the 5.........., or a 6.......... worker in a bank, store or one of the other 7.......... : if you lack 8.........., with the knowledge that you might lose your job at any time, you will never feel happy. Everybody would like a 9.......... in which he or she is guaranteed work. Nowadays, however, companies have a high turnover of staff, 10.......... new staff and 11.......... others on a weekly basis. Such companies are not popular with their workforce.

The same can be said of a job in which you are put under a lot of 12.......... and worry, a job which is so 13.......... that it takes over your life, a job where you work 14.......... and so never get to see your family or friends, or a physical job in which you do the same thing every day and end up with the modern illness that is always in the press nowadays - 15...........

With all these negative factors, it would be difficult to believe that there are any elements that make a job worthwhile. Money is, of course, the prime motivator, and everybody wants a good 16.......... But of course that is not all. The chance of 17.........., of being given a better position in a company, is a motivating factor. Likewise, 18.......... such as a free lunch or a company car, an 19.......... to make you work hard such as a regular 20.......... above the rate of inflation, 21.......... in case you fall ill and a company 22.......... program so that you have some money when you retire all combine to make a job worthwhile.

Unfortunately, it is not always easy to find all of these. There is, however, an alternative. Forget the office and the factory floor and become 23.......... and work for yourself. Your future may not be secure, but at least you will be happy.

Exercise 3. Now try this essay. Use words and expressions from the Vocabulary Bank, and any other words or expressions that you think would be relevant.

'It is more important to have a job you enjoy doing than a job which pays well'. How far do you agree with this statement? Use specific reasons and examples to support your answer.

Friends and relatives, etc

Exercise 1. Use a dictionary to check the meanings of the words in the box. Can you think of any other words and expressions to add to the list?

acquaintance • admire • adore • (steady) boyfriend • best friend
boss • bring up • brother • classmate • be close to • be fond of • cousin
discipline • empathize • empathy • encourage • encouragement
enemy • fall out with • generous • get on with • (steady) girlfriend
grandparents • have a lot in common • help • helpful • husband
influence • inspire • inspiration • kind • kinship • love • nurture
parents • partner • raise • relative • respect • roommate
see eye to eye • shared interests • sibling • sister • supervisor
support • supportive • sympathize • sympathy • teacher • wife

Exercise 2. Now try this essay. Use words and expressions from the box, and any other words or expressions that you think would be relevant.

Different people influence our lives in different ways. How? Illustrate your answer with specific examples.

Global problems and social tensions

Exercise 1. Use a dictionary to check the meanings of the words in the box. Can you think of any other words and expressions to add to the list?

charity • civil rights • cultural exchange program • culture • culture shock
differences • discriminate • discrimination • displaced people
emigrants • emigration • environment • equality • ethnic cleansing
exploit • exploitation • extremism • extremist • genocide • global village
homeless • homelessness • human rights • hunger • ignorance
immigrants • immigration • inequality • institutional racism
internally displaced • intolerance • language • migrants • nationalism
pollution • poverty • prejudice • racism • refugee • religion
religious • stateless people • study visit • terrorism • terrorist
tolerate • tolerance • UNESCO • UNHCR • UNICEF • xenophobia

Exercise 2. Now try this essay. Use words and expressions from the box, and any other words or expressions that you think would be relevant.

The world today faces a lot of problems. Outline a few of these problems and suggest some things that ordinary people could do to make the world a better place.

71

Government and politics

Exercise 1. Use a dictionary to check the meanings of the words in the box. Can you think of any other words and expressions to add to the list?

authoritarian • a bill • candidate • to canvass • the Capitol • Capitol Hill
a committee • Congress • a congressman / congresswoman • a constituent
assembly • a constitution • democratic • democracy • Democrat • to elect
an election • federal (law, tax, etc) • a governor • the House of Representatives
ideology • independence • legislation • legislature • a monarchy
opposition • parliament • a politician • a president
a prime minister • to ratify • a referendum • represent • a republic
a Republican • sanctions • the Senate • a senator • a state
a statesman / stateswoman • a technocrat • totalitarian • to vote

Exercise 2. Now try this essay. Use words and expressions from the box, and any other words or expressions that you think would be relevant.

What, in your opinion, are the most important things a government should do for its people? Support your answer with examples.

Health and exercise

Exercise 1. Use a dictionary to check the meanings of the words in the box. Can you think of any other words and expressions to add to the list?

active • aerobics • balanced diet • cholesterol • cut down on (eg, fatty foods, sugar) • disease • fall ill • fast food / junk food • fat • fiber
get fit • give up (eg, smoking) • health club • heart attack • heart disease
in good shape • in poor shape • jogging • keep fit
look after (eg, yourself, your health) • muscles • obese
on a diet • overweight • sedentary • skin problems • slim • sports center
swimming • take exercise • take up (eg, a sport) • underweight • unhealthy

Exercise 2. Now try this essay. Use words and expressions from the box, and any other words or expressions that you think would be relevant.

Too many young people these days are unhealthy and / or overweight. What advice would you give somebody who wanted to become fit and healthy?

Learning languages

Exercise 1. Use a dictionary to check the meanings of the words in the box. Can you think of any other words and expressions to add to the list?

accent • bilingual • challenging • communicate • competent
culture • dictionary • fluent • get by (in a language) • grammar
learn something parrot-fashion • lingua franca • look up (in a dictionary)
monolingual • mother tongue • multilingual • native speaker
pick up (a language) • practice • progress • pronunciation
rewarding • second language • self-access center • vocabulary

Exercise 2. Now try this essay. Use words and expressions from the box, and any other words or expressions that you think would be useful.

What are the most effective ways of learning a foreign language? Illustrate your answer with specific examples.

Movies and the theater

Exercise 1. Use a dictionary to check the meanings of the words in the box. Can you think of any other words and expressions to add to the list?

acting • action • actor / actress • atmosphere • audience • believable • big
budget • box office • cast • climax • comedy • director
drama • entertaining • exciting • funny • horror • location • movie
musical • performance • plot • romance • scenery • science fiction • screen
setting • soundtrack • special effects • stars • story • thriller • video

Exercise 2. Now try this essay. Use words and expressions from the box, and any other words or expressions that you think would be useful.

What kinds of movies do you enjoy watching, and why do you enjoy watching them? Use specific examples to explain your answer.

© Bloomsbury Publishing. For reference see *English Study Dictionary* (1-901659-61-3)

Music

Exercise 1. Use a dictionary to check the meanings of the words in the box. Can you think of any other words and expressions to add to the list?

aggressive • an album • an artist(e) • beat • blues (music) • a classic
classical music • a compilation • to compose • a composer • a concert
to conduct • a conductor • contemporary • dance music • easy listening
heavy metal • a hit • improvise • improvisation • innovative • jazz
live (adjective) • lively • lyrics • mellow • memorable • mood • opera
orchestra • percussion • pop • popular • rap • to record • recorded • reggae
relaxing • rock music • sentimental • a singer-songwriter • a soloist • strings
vocalist • vocals • wind instrument • world music

Exercise 2. Now try this essay. Use words and expressions from the box, and any other words or expressions that you think would be useful.

The music you listen to says a lot about the kind of person you are. How far do you agree with this? Use specific reasons and examples to support your answer.

Sports

Exercise 1. Use a dictionary to check the meanings of the words in the box. Can you think of any other words and expressions to add to the list?

arena • athlete • athletics • beat • coach • competitive • competitor
course • court • draw • equalize • exercise
go (swimming, jogging, climbing, etc) • hooligan • hooliganism • lose • match
opponent • opposition • pitch • play (baseball, tennis, basketball, etc)
prize • referee • score • spectator • spectator sports • sportsman /
sportswoman • stadium • support • supporter • take up (a sport) • team
team spirit • team sports • train • trainer • umpire • unite • violence • win

Exercise 2. Now try this essay. Use words and expressions from the box, and any other words or expressions that you think would be relevant.

Do you agree or disagree with the following statement? Sport plays an important role in a culture. Use specific reasons and examples to support your answer.

Exercise 1. Use a dictionary to check the meanings of the words in the box. Can you think of any other words and expressions to add to the list?

amenities • busy • character • college • community • community spirit
congestion • crime • demolish (old buildings) • eating out • environment
healthcare • historic • homeless • homelessness • hospital • housing
improve • improvement • increase • industry • job opportunities
library • livelihood • lively • local customs • mall • modern • monument
museum • neighbor • neighborhood • nightlife • noise control
park • peaceful • pollution • preserve (old buildings) • reduce • restaurants
rural • safe shopping • sports center • sports facilities • statue • street crime
theater • traditional • traffic • traffic calming • urban • zoo

Exercise 2. Now try this essay. Use words and expressions from the box, and any other words or expressions that you think would be relevant.

You have been asked for some suggestions on how to make your home town a better place. What suggestions would you make, and why?

Vocabulary record sheet

Photocopy this sheet as many times as you like, and use it to keep a record of new words and expressions that you learn. Try to build your own vocabulary bank of useful words and expressions. Keep this in a file in alphabetical order for quick reference. Review the words and expressions that you have recorded on a regular basis.

Language area *(eg, Work, Education, Idioms, Phrasal verbs, etc):*	

1. Word or expression	
2. Definition	
3. Equivalent in my language	
4. Sample sentence	

1. Word or expression	
2. Definition	
3. Equivalent in my language	
4. Sample sentence	

1. Word or expression	
2. Definition	
3. Equivalent in my language	
4. Sample sentence	

1. Word or expression	
2. Definition	
3. Equivalent in my language	
4. Sample sentence	

You may photcopy this page

GENERAL VOCABULARY (1 - 58)

Word formation: nouns (p.2)

Exercise 1

1. abolition   2. achievement   3. commitment
4. disagreement   5. emphasis   6. failure   7.
gain   8. illustration   9. justification   10.
modernization   11. objection   12.
postponement   13. refusal   14. speculation

Exercise 2

1. The vice principal was modest about his achievements at the college.

2. We requested the postponement of the meeting until next week.

3. The book has color illustrations of the birds.

4. The interviewee didn't get the job due to his refusal to wear a suit.

5. The two examiners had a disagreement over who should get the best grade.

6. The tutor placed great emphasis on the importance of completing the assignment.

7. Dennis's first attempt was a failure.

8. The dollar made a gain of five cents on the foreign exchange markets.

9. The presidential candidate made a commitment to lower taxes.

10. Do you have any objection to my smoking?

11. Increasing welfare funds was the spokesperson's justification for the tax rise.

12. There is press speculation that the governor will resign.

13. More voters were attracted to the party when it underwent modernization.

14. When did the abolition of the slave trade take place?

Word formation: adjectives (p.4)

1. Henry was very experienced in business matters.

2. Barbara is very helpful.

3. The student's two statements were contradictory.

4. The Professor's report was very controversial.

5. The government was determined to carry through the legislation.

6. The firefighter couldn't enter the room because the flames were too intense.

7. The garage is really spacious.

8. The expansion of the Internet has made the US economy prosperous.

9. Greg wasn't very enthusiastic about his schoolwork.

10. The President was extremely popular until the welfare system collapsed.

Opposites of adjectives (p.5)

Exercise 1

1. unlikely   2. illogical   3. inappropriate   4.
irresponsible   5. impatient   6. impossible   7.
dishonest   8. unexpected   9. irregular   10.
unconvincing   11. improper   12. uncertain
13. inactive   14. illiterate   15. irrelevant   16.
dissatisfied   17. unfortunate   18. disobedient
19. inaccessible   20. illegal

Exercise 2

1. unexpected   2. dissatisfied   3. inactive   4.
illegal   5. impatient   6. irrelevant   7.
improper   8. inaccessible   9. impossible   10.
illiterate   11. unfortunate   12. uncertain

Word formation: verbs (p.7)

Exercise 1

1. allow   2. experiment   3. arrange   4.
illustrate   5. calculate   6. collide   7. celebrate
8. involve   9. develop   10. limit   11. diagnose
12. maintain   13. disapprove   14. omit   15.
endorse   16. predict   17. examine   18. recover
19. exclude   20. submit

Prefixes (p.8)

autonomy = self government; being able to decide what to do yourself.   circumference = distance around the outside edge of a circle. circumvent = to avoid (something) by going around it.   cohabit = to live together as man and wife, especially when not married. cohesion = sticking together   interstate = between two states.   intermission = short time between the parts of a performance. microorganism = very small organism which can only be seen with a microscope.   microscope = instrument that enlarges things that are very small.   monopoly = system where one person or company supplies all of a product in one area without any competition.   monosyllable = word that only has one syllable (eg, dog, man, earth).   posthumous = after death. postpone = to put back to a later date or time. precondition = condition that is set in advance. predetermine = to decide in

Answer key

advance.   submarine = special type of ship that can travel under water.   subordinate = under the control of someone else. transatlantic = across the Atlantic.   transmit = to pass a disease from one person to another. unify = to join separate countries together to form one.   unique = different from everything else; the only one that exists.

Nouns (p.9)

1. valley   2. bulletin   3. fragment   4. addiction   5. justification   6. constitution   7. rehearsal   8. veteran   9. charisma   10. facet   11. investigation   12. dignitary   13. shortage   14. function   15. protein

Adjectives 1 (p.10)

1. desirable   2. genuine   3. unclear   4. emotional   5. relieved   6. sensible   7. loud   8. contagious   9. federal   10. intellectual   11. broad   12. outrageous

Adjectives 2 (p.11)

1. immediate   2. obvious   3. biased   4. random   5. judgmental   6. ideal   7. memorable   8. lasting   9. delighted   10. significant   11. advanced   12. favorable   13. persistent   14. energetic   15. effective   16. critical

Verbs 1 (p.12)

1. decline   2. exhaust   3. restore   4. overcome   5. classify   6. persuade   7. acknowledge   8. protect   9. bear   10. accuse   11. relate   12. regulate   13. benefit   14. launch

Verbs 2 (p.13)

1. c   2. e   3. h   4. i   5. l   6. a   7. k   8. d   9. b   10. g   11. f   12. j

Verbs 3 (p.14)

1. f   2. j   3. l   4. a   5. i   6. h   7. b   8. d   9. k   10. e   11. g   12. c

Prepositions (p.15)

1.   The government is underwriting ~~for~~ the costs of the exhibition.

2.   He will sue you ~~from~~ for libel.

3.   The company will meet ~~to~~ your expenses.

4.   I don't have my driver's license ~~by~~ on / with me.

5.   Can I pay later, as I'm rather short ~~for~~ of cash right now?

6.   They thought about flying here but decided to come ~~in~~ by car.

7.   We put our house ~~through~~ on the market last August.

8.   The table measures two feet by 7 feet.

9.   It's ~~from~~ against the law to drive in the dark without lights.

10.   She won ~~at~~ first prize in the art competition.

11.   We have received a letter from our daughter.

12.   He wants to spend ~~at~~ more time with his family.

13.   ~~Through~~ Under the terms of the agreement, the goods should be delivered in October.

14.   There's only a thin wall ~~from~~ between his office and mine, so I hear everything he says.

Cause and effect (p.16)

Exercise 1

1.   The boy slowed down so that his grandmother could catch up.

2.   I therefore have decided not to grant his request.

3.   The game was canceled because of the rain.

4.   It was snowing hard so we could not go for a walk.

5.   The child was very excited, and consequently could not sleep.

6.   She is only fifteen, and thus is not eligible for the over sixteens competition.

7.   We were late on account of the fog.

8.   The dog is wet because he has been in the river.

9.   Since she is ill, you cannot ask her to help you.

10.   The traffic was bumper to bumper and, as a result, Josh missed his train.

11.   I am sorry that owing to staff shortages, we cannot supply your order on time.

12.   They had to run to the theater so as not to miss the performance.

Contrast and comparison (p.17)

Exercise 1

Contrast:

alike   as   correspondingly   in common   in the same way   just as   like   similarly   similar to

Comparison:

although   different from   differ from   however   in contrast to   instead   nevertheless   on the other hand   unlike

Exercise 2

1. B   2. A   3. A   4. B

Explaining and adding more information (p.18)

1. A   2. B   3. A   4. A   5. A   6. A   7. A   8. B

Identifying the task (p.19)

1.   explain = give your reason for something.

2.   compare = to look at two things side by side to see how they are different.

3.   how = in what way.

4.   disagree = to have a different opinion.

5.   describe = to write what something is like.

6.   support = to give something your approval or favor.

7.   change = to make something different.

8.   opinion = what someone thinks about something

9.   agree = to have the same opinion or to accept an idea.

10.   why = for what reason.

11.   oppose = to be against something.

12.   prefer = to like something better than something else.

Opinion, attitude and belief (p.20)

Exercise 1

1. opinion   2. concerned   3. convinced   4. regarding   5. disapproval   6. maintains   7. reckon (in informal word which means *think* or *believe*)   8. suspect   9. doubt   10. disapprove   11. exception   12. fanatical   13. obsessive (Note: obsess*ive about* / obsess*ed with*)   14. moderates   15. conservative   16. committed   17. dedicated   18. traditional

Exercise 2

Political beliefs:

a republican   a revolutionary   left-wing   right-wing   a socialist   a royalist   a conservative   a liberal   a communist   a fascist   middle-of-the-road   an anarchist

Personal convictions and philosophies:

opinionated   pragmatic   a Muslim   an intellectual   tolerant   a moralist   narrow-minded   bigoted   open-minded   a vegan   a Buddhist   a vegetarian   dogmatic   moral   religious   a Hindu   a stoic

Time (p.21)

Exercise 1

Part 1

1. prior to (this expression is usually followed by a noun or by an -*ing* verb. For example: *Prior to visiting to country, he had to study the language*)   2. By the time   3. Formerly / Previously   4. precede   5. Previously   6. Previously / Earlier

Part 2

1. While / As / Just as (*While* is usually used to talk about long actions. *When* is usually used to talk about short actions: *While we were working, the phone rang / We were working when the phone rang*)   2. During / Throughout (*During* must always be followed by a noun. *Throughout* can be used on its own. *During the concert, I fell asleep. I slept throughout*.)   3. In the meantime / Meanwhile   4. At that very moment

Part 3

1 Following (this word is always followed by a noun. We can also say *After. Following / After the film, we went home*)   2. As soon as / Once / The minute that (these words and expressions are always followed by an action: *As soon as the lecture ended, we left the building*)   3. Afterwards

Exercise 2

The past:

in medieval times   back in the 1990's   in those days   a few decades ago   at the turn of the century   in my childhood / youth   last century   from 1996 to 1998

The past leading to the present:

ever since   over the past six weeks   lately   for the past few months

The present:

as things stand   nowadays   at this moment in

© Peter Collin Publishing. For reference see *English Study Dictionary* (1-901659-61-3)

Answer key

time   at this point in history   these days
<u>The future:</u>

for the next few weeks   one day   from now
on   over the coming weeks and months   in
another five years' time   by the end of this
year / for the foreseeable future   sooner or
later

Phrasal verbs 1 (p.22)

1. up   2. out   3. up to   4. off   5. on   6. up
with   7. down   8. out of   9. out   10. out   11.
up   12. in   13. up with   14. out   15. out   16.
into   17. on   18. behind   19. down on   20.
out   21. over   22. with   23. forward   24. back
on

Phrasal verbs 2 (p.23)

1. broke down   2. work out   3. wear off   4.
wear themselves out   5. pull through   6. sort
out   7. split up   8. showed up   9. pulled out
10. letting off   11. let you down   12. carry on
13. held up   14. fell through   15. ended up
16. carried out   17. cutting back on   18. cut
off   19. did away with   20. do up

Phrasal verbs 3 (p.25)

1. get   2. came   3. getting   4. get   5. came
6. get   7. came   8. get   9. came   10. get
11. come   12. get   13. came   14. came   15.
getting   16. comes   17. come   18. came / got
19. got   20. get

Phrasal verbs 4 (p.26)

1. look over   2. ✓   3. look after   4. give in   5.
✓   6. ✓   7. look forward to   8. ✓   9. go over
10. ✓   11. look down on   12. ✓   13. go off
14. ✓   15. ✓   16. ✓   17. give off   18. ✓   19.
look up to   20. go into

Phrasal verbs 5 (p.27)

Clues across (➔)

1. put down   4. talk them around   5. take
after   6. running up against   8. turned out
11. picked on   12. opt out   16. turned up   19.
set off   20. run up   21. made up

Clues down (⬇)

1. put aside (this has the same meaning as *set
aside*) 2. take in   3. taken in   5. turned down
7. put up with   9. stand in (also used with 'for':
I was asked to stand in for her)   10. put off

13. sets in   14. make out   15. made up   17.
ran for   18. pick up

Similar meanings 1 (p.29)

Clues across (➔)

1. prompt   3. albeit   4. settle   5. reveal   6.
detect   11. steady   12. caliber   16. obtain
17. demand   18. hasten   19. submit   20.
baffle   22. potent   24. launch   25. enrich   26.
mirror   27. robust   28. absurd

Clues down (⬇)

2. relate   3. abrupt   7. elicit   8. forbid   9.
varied   10. finite   13. convey   14. coarse   15.
narrow   16. oblige   18. handle   21. unique
22. placid   23. notion

Similar meanings 2 (p.31)

1. assert   2. toxic   3. crush   4. heighten   5.
nominal   6. lasting   7. gather   8. rigid   9.
dramatic   10. charisma   11. acclaim   12.
means   13. shallow   14. woo   15. opposition
16. negligible   17. erratic

Similar meanings 3 (p.32)

1. contemporary   2. hazardous   3. advantage
4. resolute   5. adequate   6. crucial   7. thriving
8. exemplifies   9. rudimentary   10.
indispensable   11. survey   12. tenacious   13.
inventive   14. comprehensive

The synonym for *typical* is *characteristic.*

Similar meanings 4 (p.33)

Clues across (➔)

3. replace   5. visibly   7. tedious   8. endorse
10. overtly   11. exhaust   13. uniform   14.
unravel   18. clarify   20. fertile   22. acquire
23. decline   24. recover   25. curious   26.
portray

Clues down (⬇)

1. infancy   2. promote   4. account   6.
broaden   7. triumph   9. dormant   12.
involve   15. vibrant   16. dictate   17. forfeit
19. diverse   20. fallacy   21. suspect

Similar meanings 5 (p.36)

1. acceptable   2. balanced   3. conservation
4. demonstration   5. exceptional   6.
fundamental   7. generate   8. highlight   9.
influence   10. justice   11. kudos

12. legitimate   13. magnitude   14. nevertheless   15. outlandish   16. perceive   17. quantify   18. requisite   19. somewhat   20. thorough   21. ultimatum   22. victor   23. widespread   24. xenophobic   25. yield   26. zenith

Opposites 2 (p.38)

Verbs:

1. rejected   2. denied   3. retreated   4.   5. attacked   6. demolished   7. simplified   8. abandoned   9. withdrew   10. deteriorated   11. forbade   12. rewarded   13. lowered   14. set   15. fell   16. loosened

Adjectives:

1. clear   2. easy   3. graceful   4. detrimental   5. approximate   6. innocent   7. even   8. scarce   9. flexible   10. considerable   11. crude   12. delicate   13. dim   14. compulsory   15. reluctant

Confusing words and false friends (p.39)

1. action / activity   2. advise / advice   3. effect / affect   4. appreciable / appreciative   5. assumption / presumption   6. prevent / avoid   7. beside / besides   8. shortly / briefly   9. channel / canal   10. conscious / conscientious   11. continuous / continual   12. inspect / control   13. objections / criticism   14. injury / damage / harm   15. invent / discover   16. for / during / while   17. However / Moreover   18. inconsiderable / inconsiderate   19. intolerable / intolerant   20. job / work   21. lies / lay   22. watch / look at   23. permit / permission   24. possibility / chance   25. priceless / worthless   26. principle / principal / principal / principle   27. procession / process   28. rise / raise   29. respectful / respectable   30. treat / cure

Changes (p.42)

Exercise 1

1. True   2. True   3. False: there has been an *improvement*   4. False: there has been an *increase*   5. False: there has been a *strengthening* of the dollar   6. False: there has been a *relaxation* of border controls   7. False: we're *increasing* or *building up* our stock of coal   8. True   9. False: there has been a *slight fall*   10. False: they're going to *decrease* the number   11. False: there has been a *decline*   12. False: there has been a *tightening up* of the rules   13. False: there has been a *widening* of the gap   14. True   15. False: there has been

a *downward* trend   16. True   17. True   18. True   19. True   20. False: Americans want to *broaden* their horizons.

Most of the words in this task can be <u>verbs</u> as well as <u>nouns</u>. Use a dictionary to check which ones.

Addition, equation and conclusion (p.44)

Exercise 1.

Addition:
and   along with   as well as   also   too   in addition   besides   what's more   furthermore   moreover   along with (this could also be equation)

Equation:
equally   likewise   similarly   in the same way   correspondingly

Conclusion:
to sum up briefly   it can be concluded that   to conclude   in brief   thus   to summarize   therefore

Exercise 2.

1. Furthermore / Moreover / In addition / What's more (this is less formal than the other expressions)   2. As well as / Besides   3. Likewise / Similarly / In the same way (the verbs in both sentences - ie, *respect* - are the same and refer to the same thing, so we can use a word of equation here)   4. As well as / Along with   5. In addition   6. Likewise / Similarly   7. Likewise / In the same way / Correspondingly   8. In brief   9. It can be concluded that   10. Therefore (To *sum up*, To *conclude* and To *summarise* are usually used to conclude longer pieces of writing - eg, at the end of an essay. *Thus* is slightly more formal than *therefore*, but has the same meaning)

Note: It is important that you are familiar with the way these words and expressions are used, including the other words in a sentence that they 'work' with. Use a dictionary to look up examples of these words and expressions, and keep a record of them to refer to the next time you use them.

Working words (p.45)

1. to / no / of   2. ago / used or had / These   3. even   4. Between / almost or about or over   5. most or some / near   6. be / on   7. Unless / on or for   8. at / knowing or realizing / would   9.

Answer key

spite / managed   10. as / anyone   11. This / of   12. who / just or recently   13. with / made   14. by / had   15. the / where   16. give / until / two / these   17. which / one / whole or entire   18. least / more / because or as or since / had   19. what / from / else

Spelling (p.46)

The words in **bold** are spelt correctly.

1.

Apart from **condemning** tobacco companies and **raising** the price of cigarettes, the **government's** antismoking **campaign** has failed to have any long-term **effects**, and the only people **benefiting** from it are the Internal Revenue **service**. Meanwhile, the National Health Service says it may refuse to treat **persistent** smokers. Of course, this hasn't prevented the big **tobacco companies** spending vast amounts of money on **advertising**.

2.

It is **arguable** whether good **pronunciation** is more important than good **grammar** and **vocabulary**. **Conscientious** students balance their **acquisition** of these skills, **hoping** to **achieve** both fluency and **accuracy**. Teachers should **encourage their** students to practice all the relevant language skills.

3.

It is **becoming** increasingly **difficult** for many to find decent **accommodations** in Los Angeles at a price they can afford. To put it **simply**, most people just don't have the **necessary** funds. **Organizations** such as Home Front can offer **advice**, but it widely agreed that the situation is no longer **manageable**. The fact that the LA city council is building cheap, **temporary** housing for lower-paid **professionals** is the only official **acknowledgment** of this problem.

Presenting an argument (p.47)

Exercise 1

The best order is: 1. A   2. H   3. K   4. M   5. E   6. G   7. B   8. J   9. F   10. O   11. L   12. N   13. L   14. D   15. I   16. P

When you are asked to present an argument (eg, in an essay), you should always look at it from two sides, giving reasons why you agree and disagree before reaching a conclusion. It is usually best to present your strongest argument in favor of something just before you write the conclusion.

Other words and expressions that you might find useful include:

I believe that   despite this   in spite of this   also   thirdly   I think   finally   in conclusion   nonetheless   admittedly   on the contrary   at any rate   notwithstanding   for all that   even if

Idioms and colloquialisms 1 (p.48)

1. about   2. ahead   3. along   4. once   5. all   6. As   7. least   8. most   9. out   10. short   11. far   12. tied   13. up   14. best   15. mind   16. fed   17. cheer   18. other   19. gear   20. hold   21. ground   22. fault   23. being   24. hand   25. hand   26. rid   27. mind   28. worse   29. wonder   30. head

Idioms and colloquialisms 2 (p.50)

1. I don't mind   2. Not again!   3. I couldn't agree more   4. No way!   5. Let me sleep on it.   6. I'm afraid it turns me off.   7. Get a life!   8. I couldn't care less!   9. Way to go!   10. Go for it!   11. Not at all   12. Never mind, it can't be helped.   13. Sure, why not?   14. How's it going?   15. How should I know? (or I couldn't care less)   16. What a drag!   17. You bet!   18. I'll give it all I've got.   19. I'm used to it.   20. What do you have in mind?

Idioms and colloquialisms 3 (p.52)

These are the correct responses to the first sentences:

A.

1. I'd be glad to (this is a polite way of agreeing to do something).   2. Be my guest (this is a polite way of giving somebody permission to do something).   3. A little bird told me (we say this when we don't want to say who said something to us).   4. My lips are sealed (we say this when we promise to keep a secret, or when we refuse to tell someone a secret).   5. I'm keeping my fingers crossed (we say this when we are hoping that something will happen).   6. Rather you than me (this means that we are glad we are not doing something that somebody else is).   7. Fire away, I'm all ears (this means that we are ready to listen to something).   8. Now you're talking (we say this when somebody suggests something that is more acceptable or enjoyable than something

84

else they have already suggested). 9. I'm having second thoughts (this means that we will probably change our mind about something we have already agreed to). 10. That'll be the day (this means that we don't believe something will happen)

B.

1. Oh, this is one me (we say this when we are offering to pay for something). 2. Congratulations (this is another way of saying 'Well done'). 3. I'd love to (we say this when we are accepting an offer to do something) 4. You're welcome (this is another way of saying 'Not at all' or 'Don't mention it'). 5. Thanks. Make yourself at home (this is an expression we use when somebody visits our house). 6. Hold on (an informal expression which means 'Wait'). 7. Yes. Take care and keep in touch (an expression we use when we will not see somebody for a while). 8. Couldn't be better (this means that we are very well). 9. I'd rather you didn't (this is a polite way of telling somebody that you don't want them to do something). 10. Oh, that's too bad (this is another way of saying 'Hard luck', 'Bad luck' or 'Tough luck', and we use it to sympathize with someone)

C.

1. How's it going? (an informal way of asking somebody if something is going well or badly) 2. I'll say (when we agree completely with somebody) 3. Not on your life! (an informal way of saying that we would never do something) 4. That's a load off my mind. (when we are suddenly no longer worried about something that was troubling us. We can also say 'That's a weight off my mind') 5. Well, keep it to yourself (don't tell anyone else, usually because something is, or should be, a secret) 6. Sure thing (an informal way of saying we agree to do something) 7. Of course, take a seat ('Take a seat' means 'Sit down') 8. Well, take it easy. Don't kill yourself. (these are informal ways of telling somebody not to work too hard, or to calm down, relax) 9. Cheer up. It's not the end of the world (we use the first expression when we want somebody to be happier, we use the second expression to tell them that things are not as bad as they seem).

Idioms and colloquialisms 4 (p.54)

1. S 2. Q 3. R 4. E 5. V 6. A 7. B 8. G 9. N 10. O 11. U 12. F 13. P 14. K

15. M 16. T 17. J 18. H 19. D 20. I 21. L 22. C

Idioms and colloquialisms 5 (p.56)

1. candle 2. worms 3. bull 4. nose 5. blind 6. track 7. pressed 8. weather 9. blue 10. record 11. ground 12. ice 13. air 14. shop 15. ground 16. close 17. picture 18. name 19. world 20. strings 21. played 22. red 23. good 24. out 25. ground

TOPICS (59 - 70)

Children and the family (p.60)

1. formative 2. divorced 3. brought up 4. foster family 5. authoritarian / strict 6. upbringing 7. running wild 8. adolescence 9. juvenile delinquency 10. responsible 11. siblings 12. well-adjusted 13. lenient 14. overprotective 15. nuclear 16. single-parent 17. dependants 18. extended

Education (p.61)

1. skills 2 / 3. literacy / numeracy (in either order) 4. kindergarten / elementary school 5. elementary 6. secondary 7. discipline 8. pass 9. qualifications 10. acquire 11. physical education 12. graduate 13. higher 14. degree 15. subject 16. graduate school 17. doctorate 18. evening class 19. distance learning course 20. online course 21. opportunity

Food and diet (p.62)

1. fast food 2 / 3. minerals / vitamins (in either order) 4 / 5. fat / carbohydrates (in either order) 6. malnutrition 7. scarcity 8. harvest 9. balanced diet 10. fiber 11. fat / cholesterol 12. calories 13. genetically modified 14. organic 15 / 16. salmonella / listeria (in either order) 17. food poisoning

The media (p.63)

1. coverage 2. current affairs 3. reporters 4. journalists 5. tabloids 6. broadcasts 7. cable 8. Internet 9. websites 10. download 11 / 12 information / entertainment (in either order) 13. gutter press 14. invasion of privacy 15. paparazzi 16. libel 17. checkbook journalism 18. unscrupulous 19. Internet / web 20. information overload 21. logging on

22. censorship   23. freedom of the press

Money and finance (p.64)

1. borrow   2. loan   3. income   4. expenditure   5. overdraft   6. cost of living
7. inflation   8. economize   9. savings   10. on credit   11. exorbitant   12. save   13. reductions   14. bargain   15. discount   16. invest   17. stocks   18. shares

Nature and the environment (p.65)

1. fossil fuels   2. acid rain   3. greenhouse gases / CFC gases   4. global warming
5. rainforest   6. contaminated   7. emissions / gases   8. poaching   9. endangered species
10. ecosystem   11. recycle   12. biodegradable
13. genetically modified   14. organic
15. unleaded fuel   16. environmentalists
17. conservation programes   18. factory farming   19. ocean

On the road (p.66)

1 / 2. injuries / fatalities (in either order)
3. speeding   4. speed limit   5. drunk- driving
6. pedestrians   7. crosswalks   8. traffic light
9 / 10. congestion / pollution (in either order)
11. black spot   12. transportation strategy
13. Traffic calming   14. Park and ride
15. traffic-free zone / pedestrian mall
16. bicycle lanes   17. subsidized   18. fines
19. dominate   20. traffic school

Science and technology (p.67)

1. discovered   2. life expectancy   3. innovations / inventions   4. breakthrough   5. invented   6. Internet   7. e-mail   8. research
9. technophiles   10. technophobes   11. cybernetics   12. nuclear engineering   13. safeguards   14. genetic engineering   15. analyzed   16. experiment

City life and country life (p.68)

1. metropolis   2. cosmopolitan   3. urban   4. amenities / facilities   5. cultural events   6. infrastructure   7. commuters   8. Central Business District   9. rush hour / peak periods
10. congestion / traffic jams   11. pollution
12. cost of living   13. construction sites   14. population explosion   15. drug abuse / street crime   16. inner city   17. rural   18. prospects
19. productive land / cultivation / arable land
20. urban sprawl   21. environment

Travel (p.69)

1. travel agency   2. package tour   3. independent travelers   4. visas   5. check in
6. coach class   7. disembark   8. mass tourism
9. all-inclusive   10. ecotourism   11. refugees
12. internally displaced   13. economic migrants   14. expatriates   15. culture shock
16. immigration   17. persona non grata   18. deported   19. checking in   20. excursion

Work (p.70)

1. employees   2. unskilled   3. semiskilled   4. blue-collar   5. manufacturing industries   6. white-collar   7. service industries   8. job security   9. steady job   10. hiring   11. firing
12. pressure   13. demanding   14. unsociable hours   15. stress   16. salary   17. promotion
18. benefits   19. incentive   20. raise   21. sick pay   22. pension   23. self-employed